PRAISE FOR

THE SIXTH MAN

"The best basketball memoir since Bill Russell's *Go Up for Glory.* . . . A sports memoir for the ages."   —*Booklist* (starred review)

"Iguodala's story is a compelling and important one that provides a glimpse into what people of color face, from little boys to the height of stardom, in a country 'designed to wreak absolute havoc on the confidence of black people.'"   —Shelf Awareness

"A true insider's perspective of the Warriors' championship teams."
—*Library Journal*

"A fascinating look at the intersection of class, race and basketball."
—*Axios*

"A riveting read by one of the NBA's sharpest minds."   —*Forbes*

"A deeply personal look at Iguodala's life growing up in Springfield, Ill., with his single mother and brother, who he says taught him how to be a defender early on. In reflective, conversational prose, Iguodala recounts his early awareness of segregation and racism, the strength and influence of the strong women in his life (and later, coaches), and his gradual realization of how to best harness his intelligence, ambition and drive."   —*Datebook*

THE SIXTH MAN

═ A MEMOIR ═

ANDRE IGUODALA

WITH CARVELL WALLACE

BLUE RIDER PRESS

New York

blue
rider
press

BLUE RIDER PRESS
An imprint of Penguin Random House LLC
penguinrandomhouse.com

Previously published as a Blue Rider Press hardcover in 2019
First Blue Rider Press trade paperback printing: June 2020
Copyright © 2019 by Andre Iguodala

Blue Rider Press is a registered trademark and its colophon is a trademark
of Penguin Random House LLC

The Library of Congress has catalogued the hardcover edition of this book as follows:

Names: Iguodala, Andre, author.
Title: The Sixth Man: A Memoir / Andre Iguodala.
Description: New York: Blue Rider Press, 2019. |
Identifiers: LCCN 2018047034 | ISBN 9780525533986 (hardback) |
ISBN 9780525534006 (ebook)
Subjects: LCSH: Iguodala, Andre. | African American basketball
players—Biography. | Basketball players—United States—Biography. |
Olympic athletes—United States—Biography. | Golden State Warriors
(Basketball team). | BISAC: BIOGRAPHY & AUTOBIOGRAPHY /
Sports. | SPORTS & RECREATION / Basketball. |
BIOGRAPHY & AUTOBIOGRAPHY / Personal Memoirs.
Classification: LCC GV884.I76 A3 2019 | DDC 796.323092 [B]—dc23
LC record available at https://lccn.loc.gov/2018047034

Blue Rider Press trade paperback ISBN: 9780525533993

Printed in the United States of America
1 3 5 7 9 10 8 6 4 2

BOOK DESIGN BY LAURA K. CORLESS

To young fella, stay black!

CONTENTS

INTRODUCTION

I t was the whole summer that changed me. Of course, everything changes you, but still there are moments that do it more than others, moments where life unfolds itself to you, peels away its layers piece by piece until you realize there is an entire universe of possibility right there staring, unblinking, back at you. That summer, that entire universe of possibility was in, of all places, Orlando, Florida. Disney World to be precise. It was the farthest away I'd ever been from my home in Springfield, Illinois. I was about to be a senior in high school.

It was 2001. The Jay-Z song "Izzo (H.O.V.A.)" came out and we couldn't get enough of it. Our basketball team was bumping it that whole Florida trip, and it was the first thing I really bonded over with the Chicago kids, the first thing that made me feel like I belonged. Compared to them, I was a hayseed, this skinny kid with big ears from Springfield, Illinois. They used to tease me. My clothes were behind, my slang was behind, half the stuff they were talking about, I had no idea what it was. I tried to blend in, but I couldn't. It was too obvious that I was a small-town kid playing on an Amateur Athletic Union (AAU) team with kids from the city.

When you come from a town like Springfield, you just don't know how you compare to the entire world that is out there. That's the hardest part. You have no point of reference. Then all of a sudden you find yourself on a bus in Florida, on the way to a national basketball tournament at a place called Disney World. You are looking out the window at vast boulevards and palm trees seemingly weighted down by the sweat in the air; at strip malls and long, tall grass fields for miles; at a surface so hot and so foreign to you that it might as well have been Mercury.

I didn't understand what was happening in my life. The ground was moving beneath my feet. I had entered the summer thinking I was a pretty good high school basketball player. But mostly I just loved the game. I loved feeling the emotions of a contest, how things would ebb and flow with a team over two halves. I loved sensing where my teammates were going to be cutting, firing the ball to a guy with a crisp pass and watching him catch it and lay it in all in one unbroken movement. I liked playing with my best friend on the squad, Rich McBride. He was from Springfield too, but he was already more of a national name than I was. Basketball magazines had him highly ranked, and he had started on the varsity squad as a freshman. He was a star, a big enough deal that everyone took him seriously. I always felt like I was the second guy when he was around. Not quite as cool, not quite as famous.

I just liked to practice, I just liked to get better. I just liked to take shots alone in the gym until my legs threatened to give out. I just liked to watch games from the sidelines, trying to understand what every player was doing, what every coach was thinking. I just wanted to be as good as I could, learn as much as I could. I just wanted to earn my place.

But weird things were happening. I had gotten an invitation to a Nike Camp earlier that summer and that was next level. Nike Camp was only for the top players in the country. I didn't think I was among that class, for sure, but nonetheless there I was. I went there and tried to do my best. Keep it fundamental, don't make any mistakes, try not to get beat. I left not knowing how I had done, but within a month I had been contacted by coaches of Division I basketball programs around the country. Nolan Richardson at Arkansas, Gary Williams at Maryland, Roy Williams from Kansas, Lute Olson from Arizona. It was surreal. OK, so maybe I was going to be good enough to go to college, but still I was just the second fiddle on my own AAU team.

Then there was Peach Jam, another tournament we played earlier in the summer. I got there and saw some of the best players I had ever seen in my life. In particular there was a dude named Rashad Mc-Cants, a six-foot-four guard out of a prep school in New Hampshire. He was, and I have no doubt about this, one of the top five basketball players I've ever seen. On any level. Period. To this day, I believe that is true. Yet he only played in the league for three years. How is that possible? The answer to that question is not something I would learn until much later in life. I would learn that the higher up you go in this game, the more replaceable you become. I would learn that being the best was not a guarantee of a career, that a career was made of myriad things, of small, boring things. Of good agents and early morning workouts. Of medical procedures and yoga and nutritionists. Of sleep hygiene and the ability to tamp your emotions down so hard that they first become stones and then diamonds that you only reveal when there are three seconds on the clock and you are down by two points and you have to see, understand, and predict the movements of ten men on a basketball court at one time, while 45,000 people are screaming at you. A career is made of these things. It is made of broken fingers and trade rumors and coaches you can't quite trust, and the occasional referee who reminds you a little too much of the police officers that stalked your neighborhood when you were a kid, glowering at you and your friends as though you were dangerous animals escaped from captivity rather than children—a look that gives you a cold chill, a fight-or-flight response that will lie dormant and coiled and always ready to spring at the base of your spine for the rest of your life.

I didn't know any of this yet. I was a kid. I liked Jay-Z. I wanted to fit in. I kept growing out of my clothes. I didn't want to embarrass myself or my team at the tournament. I liked making people laugh. I used to take the tobacco out of one of our assistant coach's cigarettes and put it back in his pack, and when he lit it up, the whole thing went up in flames. We thought it was hilarious. He used to get so pissed. I had no idea people were obsessed with their cigarettes like that.

At Peach Jam we made it to the final four, but we didn't win. I felt like everything in that last game was happening too fast for me. Dudes were too quick, too sharp. I didn't know how to keep up, and it felt like I couldn't get over the hump. It was disappointing. I had done my best but it wasn't good enough. The summer was moving along. I had been to Nike Camp, I had played OK at Peach Jam, but I still felt like I was swimming upstream.

At the Disney World tournament, we were in the semifinals against some East Coast team, maybe from DC or Baltimore. I wasn't yet used to having full-on confidence when I played against kids from other cities, but I was used to drafting off the confidence of those

Chicago boys on my team. Collectively we didn't feel like we needed to back down from *anybody*, no matter where they came from. But now it seemed that guys were actually keying in on me. I could see the team and coach looking at me during time-outs. When I got the ball, there would be a dude in my chest, sometimes two, like immediately. It started to dawn on me that, for some reason, these guys were treating me as though I was the man on the team. In Springfield, while playing on junior varsity and varsity teams, I had seen guys double-team me, make me the priority, but it was not hard to manage there. Down here in Florida, however, it was a whole different ball game. These were seventeen-, eighteen-year-old guys, elite guys, guys who were about to start at Division I programs. This was not high school basketball. It was something different. When they were on me, I couldn't breathe. These guys on me were getting after it, dogging my every twitch.

We managed to hang around in that game, never getting too far behind, but I was not able to produce the kind of offense I was used to. We got to the end of the game and there were three or four seconds left on the clock. They scored, we were down two. We called a time-out so we could advance the ball to the other end of the court. There wasn't much to say during the time-out. I mean, as good as we all were, this was still AAU. No one was drawing up elaborate plays. It was basically just getting the ball, going down and shooting. We had this one white kid on the team, a smart dude, very fundamentally sound. Coach drew up a play for him to get the ball and make something happen. As we were walking back onto the court, he turned to me and said, "Andre, I'm coming to you, man. Be ready."

Me? Was I the guy that teams go to when they're down two with seconds on the clock?

Dude got the ball, took one dribble, found me away from the

basket. I had to be like thirty-five feet out, if I remember correctly, damn near half-court it felt like. I didn't think. I didn't hope. I didn't wish. I just shot. It was so simple. There was no distance between me and anything in the world. I just shot the ball as naturally as if I were taking a breath. As I shot it, a defender was flying toward me, kind of brushed me a touch, and I fell backward out of my own momentum. All I saw was him standing over me, and behind him I could just barely make out the ball going through the net.

Swoosh.

Everybody was going crazy. You don't even know what you're doing in that moment, you're just jumping and running and screaming. Hugging whoever. We were teenage boys in Florida in the summer of 2001, covered in sweat, a million miles away from a classroom, jumping up and down, waving our arms, and running like kindergartners at an unsupervised slumber party, hopped up on bottomless bowls of Halloween candy.

Eventually we remembered ourselves enough to shake hands with the other team, and I just remember one of their players saying, "Damn, we had him shut down the whole game!" It was still hard to believe they were talking about me.

The next game, we played a team with JJ Redick on it, who was already known as one of the best high school shooters in the country. I was on him defensively and had to lock him down as well as I could. It was the most complete game I had played up until that point. It was something else, something beyond what I was used to. It came easily. Years later my teammate Klay Thompson would describe this feeling so simply. "You feel like you can do anything," he said to me. That's it. You feel like you can do anything.

That summer might have been the first time I had that feeling, an invisible power, a simplicity, a oneness that made you capable of everything, a slowing of the game, a strengthening of the muscles, a disappearing of the aches and pains. Baskets become wide as barns, defenders become small as children. I would get that feeling for a moment that summer and it would open up the entire universe of possibility for me, a universe where in the very far distance I could make out a future. Championships and trophies. Commercials and investments. Interviews and cars. Olympics and bank accounts. Tech conferences and, yes, even a book. What I could see was as far away from Springfield, Illinois, as anything could ever be.

But if I was going to have it, I was going to have to leave everything behind. I was going to have to cut loose every single thing that held me back. I was going to have to hurt. And, even then, that feeling was going to be fleeting. It was going to come ever so briefly in moments like fireflies lighting up the summer sky before disappearing again. Most of the time that feeling would be eclipsed by confusions and complexities and difficulties and frustrations more dark and thorny and unwieldy than my 2001-summer-in-Disney-World-Florida self could have ever imagined, let alone understood. Most of the time I would spend looking, once again, for that freedom.

01

Early Lessons

The Midwest makes a certain kind of person. Even-keeled, simple, and without drama. Where I come from, you get all four seasons with all their fullness and all their difficulty. The winters humble you. There are no mountains or tall buildings to stop the winds, so they just come at you like you don't matter. It's so cold that you can feel it in your bones. You think your skin is going to break, and your body seems like something not too well designed for this intensity. Winters in the Midwest make you feel small, and they help you know your place. You can't compete with the winter and wind out there. You are just a person. Your body is all you have and it's not much.

But the summers kill you another way. The air is blanket-thick and lays on top of you like it wants to suffocate you. Mosquitoes, gnats, and flies dog your every move. Your clothes get soaked with sweat, dry up, and get soaked again six different times a day, and you get used to the feeling of being dried up and salty, and pounding pop and Kool-Aid, sucking on ice cubes or freezy pops. You never feel 100 percent right in the summer, and you never feel 100 percent right in the winter. You never feel right at all. You learn not to expect too much. You just get used to it.

My hometown of Springfield, Illinois, has a population of 115,000, and about 20,000 of those people are black. And from the perspective of my early childhood, the black world was the only world there was. Officially, Springfield is not a segregated town, but officialities don't matter in race. Springfield is segregated. It always has been, and it always will be. That's not accidental. In 1908 Springfield experienced one of the most violent and intense race riots in American history. Two black men were accused of rape and attempted rape of a white woman. The town sheriff transferred the men to a jail in another town to avoid mob justice, but 5,000 white citizens nonetheless decided to attack the black neighborhood as a whole. They killed fifteen black people, lynched two, and burned bodies in public. A baby died of smoke inhalation. An eighty-year-old wealthy black business owner, himself a friend of Abraham Lincoln's, had his throat slit by a white vegetable merchant. By the time it was done, there had been what today would be over $4 million in property damage, including attacks on white businesses that were thought to be too friendly to black customers. Despite taking place in a northern town, the Springfield Race Riot was the primary reason for the founding of the NAACP. The woman who was said to have led the mob, Kate Howard, wrote that after visiting the South, she was inspired by the efficiency of Jim Crow segregation's ability to "teach the Negro where he belonged." She killed herself before she could be brought to trial. The woman who launched the rape accusations, Mabel Hallam, later admitted that she had made up the story to cover for her husband's physical abuse. She was never convicted of a crime.

A town doesn't fix itself after a thing like that, unless the people really work very hard to address it. And Springfield didn't. The Illinois General Assembly didn't even formally acknowledge the event had occurred until 2008. Instead what happened is that over the generations, this trauma just seeped back into the skin and calcified into the town's DNA. Black people stayed on one side, white people stayed on the other. Both remained insular and suspicious of the other. By the time my generation came around, things were just that way, subtly but persistently. It never occurred to any of us that they didn't have to be that way. In Springfield it rarely occurred to most people that things could be any other way.

We had our own world, the black side, and within that world I had my own little community. My mother, my brother, my grandmother, all my cousins, my rec league coaches, and me. That was Andre's world. I remember the summers, waves of heat rising up off of the asphalt, and the fields had grasses as tall as my head.

My grandmother's name is Poletha Webster, and she was the biggest influence on my early life. She was a tough and loving woman, and I can still see her standing in the sun, tending to her vegetable garden, which she did with great care while I ran around the house making games out of everything. She cared for that garden like it was her lifeblood, and from it she could produce the most beautiful vegetables you've ever seen. Perfect tomatoes and Technicolor-ripe squashes that she would use to make pies and casseroles. Sweet peas and strawberries. Her hands were always busy, and those early summer afternoons were quiet and magical for me, a small child, with my grandmother beside me and my hands in the dirt, warmed by the sun.

That peace, however, came at a price. You had better keep your behavior buttoned up and not cross Poletha. She was always loving, she could be sweet when she needed to be, but if you ended up on her bad side, you would regret it.

I remember a day when I learned that lesson the hard way. My grandmother's house functioned as a neighborhood foster home, and she took in kids whose parents couldn't care for them for some reason or another. So along with me, my brother, and my cousins, there were always three or four kids staying with her. I never knew exactly what their stories were—maybe they had parents who were locked up or on drugs. But whatever their stories were before, my grandmother would take them in, receive a small stipend from the county, and make them, for as long as they lasted, part of our family. We ate together and played together all day long.

One afternoon when I was about eight years old, I was outside shooting basketballs in the rickety old hoop she had next to her house. All of us were outside, with some of the kids playing in the field next to us and others running around in the garden. But a lot of times I preferred to be alone. Just me and a basketball and the hoop. My grandmother had been tending to chores all morning—cleaning, hanging up laundry outside—stopping occasionally to yell at one of us to quit acting up or stop menacing the other kids with a stick, but mostly leaving us to our own devices. I guess one of the foster kids had peed in the bed the night before, so she had pulled one of her old mattresses out to let it air-dry. She placed it down next to the house and went on about her business.

Obviously, a mattress outside is just too interesting for most kids to completely ignore, so one by one they started drifting over to it and jumping on it. Next they were doing flips and Superman dives, and pretty soon they were making a game of it, seeing who could push who off the mattress. They were yelling at me, "Come on,

Andre! Come play with us!" It did look like fun, and as one of the youngest, I always felt cool whenever I was included in what everyone else was doing. But then I thought about it. She hadn't said so *specifically*, but I had a pretty strong feeling that my grandmother would not be pleased if she saw what was going down. As tempting as it was, I made a decision to stick to my basketball.

But when you're a kid, things like this are hard to resist. Everybody looked like they were having so much fun bouncing around and giggling that, after a while, curiosity got the better of me. Slowly but surely, I drifted over there to start jumping on the mattress too. It seemed like I had been over there for less than, I swear to God, three whole seconds before my grandmother appeared from nowhere, like a damn ghost. She was right up on me. All the kids had scattered and I was left. Caught red-handed. I tried to explain, the way kids do, that it wasn't my fault—I was just shooting hoops and minding my own business. *They* were the ones who started it! But she wasn't buying it. She just looked at me and said, "You were shooting that ball in that hoop, over there? But when I found you, you were over here, where there ain't no hoop?" I didn't have an answer. Every cousin, kid, friend, whoever who was out there that afternoon, caught a whooping from my grandmother, including me. That was one of my first life lessons and maybe the most important one: if I just keep my head down and focus on basketball, I'm generally better off.

Poletha Webster came from Arkansas. First, she moved to Kansas City with my mother's father. He was a man I met only once. I was so young at the time that I don't even remember saying anything to him, just seeing this tall, dark-skinned man and being told that he was my mother's father. I believe Poletha lived in Kansas City for a good while. In fact, my great aunt Jean lived in Kansas City, Missouri, until she passed away in 2017. When my mother was in high school, they moved to

Springfield. Poletha had divorced her first husband, my mother's father, and moved to Springfield, with my mother in tow, to be with her second husband. I never met him either. By the time I was born, Poletha was on her own. I think she preferred it that way.

I was at Evergreen Terrace for only a short part of my childhood. Soon she moved to a two-story house on Carpenter Street in a working-class section of Springfield. That house became the center of my childhood. My mother, brother, and I lived in the attic from the time I was in early elementary school until my mother got married when I was in middle school.

My childhood was solid, safe, and fun, and in some ways even beautiful. I was a mama's boy. I never wanted to be away from her. That was my first true identity. Everybody used to tease me about it, but if my mom was gone for one night, I couldn't last. I would be in a puddle of tears the entire time.

The closest person in age to me was my brother, Frank. He's just eighteen months older. You would think two boys growing up together that closely would be best friends, but that's not exactly how it was. Frank and I were always so fundamentally different that we formed separate lives starting from a very early age. To be entirely honest, it's only recently that we started to really like each other.

We had such a big and involved extended family that Frank and I didn't need to be that close. It was kind of like in the movie *Soul Food*, and Grandma was the center of it all. My one aunt was always over at the house, and she had three kids. My other aunt was always over as well, and she had two kids, plus various foster kids and neighborhood kids would be drifting in and out. So when you added it all up, that was like ten or eleven kids running around the house at all times. And my cousins were not like regular cousins: they were more like brothers and sisters. It seemed like I spent every day with them. I had two cousins I especially rocked with because we were even closer in age than my brother and I were.

Frank also had a difficult personality. He was much more defiant, much more troubled than I was. Everything I learned about keeping my head down and flying under the radar was completely absent for him in his early years. He was ready to challenge anyone and anything at any time. He didn't like to lose, and he didn't like to follow rules. And nothing seemed to bother him. Punishments, whoopings—he just didn't care. He would always say, "So what? It just hurts for a little and then it's done." He was always directed to do whatever he wanted, however he wanted, whenever he wanted. He was a kid driven entirely by his own will. Sometimes I admired that. Sometimes it was a pain in the ass.

Frank was the kind of guy who saw things his way and that's the way it was. He had a hard time seeing things from another person's perspective. For one thing, he used to cheat. At everything. Blatantly. It didn't matter what the game was, he would just boldly cheat and then deny it. I remember playing one-on-one basketball with him at the playground when we were kids. Every time I had the ball, he'd hack me up, slap my arm, damn near tackle me. He called it "playing physical," but really it was unadulterated fouling. And when I tried to call him out, he would flat-out deny it. "What, man? I barely touched you." This drove me crazy. I knew he fouled me. He knew he fouled me. But he would make me doubt myself. I had to play extremely physically just to get a shot off. At times what we did probably looked from the outside closer to football than basketball. The other thing he did consistently was change the score in the middle of a game. Every time I took the lead or tied it up, here goes Frank: "Nah, bruh. I'm still ahead. It's eight to seven right now."

There wasn't really anything I could do about it. Sometimes I felt like throwing the ball as hard as I could, storming off the court, and punching a hole in a wall. But I knew he'd just call me a baby for that. So it made me want to beat him as badly as I could. The angrier I got, the more focused I became. What started out as a game between two brothers would suddenly feel to me like a life-or-death struggle for my whole existence. I tried to pride myself on being calm and even-keeled when I was growing up. I wasn't trying to be one of those out-of-control types. I saw what out-of-control anger did to people and I wanted no part of it. But playing basketball with Frank made me angry in a way that nothing else did. I knew I had to keep it in check because he was my big brother. So I swallowed it and learned how to use it to play. It was like a performance-enhancing drug. One hit of it and suddenly I could run faster, jump higher, and get to the hoop quicker. I just wanted to prove to him that there was nothing he could do to stop me. Over time I would come to regard the entire world like that. But I learned it first from my brother.

Maybe the biggest difference between Frank and me wasn't how we were made but what we did with it. We were both combative, energetic, and incredibly competitive. But for some reason, I could always find a way to channel these things. I was an active kid, both mentally and physically. Sometimes it seemed like everything was happening in my head faster than it was in everyone else's head, and I often felt restless and jumpy. But I learned pretty early that if you could just focus on getting something done, especially if your goal was to do it better than other people could, you could stay out of trouble. So that's what I tried to do.

School came particularly easy to me. I've always loved sports and I've always loved reading, and I suspect that both of these things came from my mother. Reading was simply a nonnegotiable in my house. If you weren't reading, you weren't achieving. But I could find ways to turn even reading into a competitive act. In elementary school there was a summer reading program where you got a sticker for each book you read, and if you got a certain number of stickers, at the end of the summer you got a pizza party. Once I found out about that, it was all the way on. Just knowing that other kids were somewhere else trying to get stickers motivated me to push myself. I couldn't stand the idea of someone thinking they were better than I was at reading. I spent that whole summer engulfed in books, flying through them at lightning speed. You better believe that, come fall, I was the first kid in attendance at that pizza function.

The other thing we read at home was the newspaper. This also came from my mom. She insisted on it. She made sure we were keeping ourselves educated. If we ever had the nerve to try to complain that we were bored (which we rarely did), she'd toss the newspaper in our direction before we could finish the sentence. In this way, I learned to be interested in world affairs, business, culture, and media. I learned how stories were told and how media and journalism work, and I was always fascinated about the idea of someone ending up in the paper. Most kids wanted to be on TV, but when I was little I thought the most famous you could possibly be was to have your picture in Springfield's *State Journal-Register.*

I thought that reading the newspaper as a kid was perfectly normal until I was about twelve years old and visiting a faraway older cousin. My brother and I were sitting around the living room of our cousin's house, sharing sections of the paper, when my cousin's boyfriend walked in the room, stopped and stared at us, and then laughed. "What the hell are you guys doing?"

"Umm . . . reading the paper?"

"You *do* that?"

"You *don't?*"

That was the first time it occurred to me that Frank and I were being raised in a way that was different from a lot of the people around us. It's almost like we had to be a part of two worlds. Among kids on the playground and on the court, we had to be cool, athletic, and, if not aggressive, at least not ready to back down if confronted. But at home we were well educated, well mannered, well taken care of, and critical thinkers. When I got out of Springfield, I would find that there were a lot of players in college and the NBA who learned to balance these two ways of being, but in Springfield I felt pretty alone.

Reading aside, what we did most as kids involved running. One of the best things about Springfield was that you could find an open field just about anywhere. And we found them everywhere. We would just make up games. Play hide-and-seek, stickball, tag. My cousins and I and the other neighborhood kids had this long block radius that was ours. And there was a field two doors down from my grandmother's house. We'd play baseball out there, making the bases out of sticks and boards and bricks that we found. We got neighborhood football games going during football season. There were so many of us kids that there was always activity going on. On summer evenings we would exhaust ourselves, playing until the very last light was in the sky and the crickets and cicadas could be heard singing in the trees and fields. And in the fall and winter we'd bundle up and run through the snow, chasing each other, playing touch football on the frozen dirt, pausing only to warm our hands with our breath between plays. Life was fairly simple, and it was fairly good then. We had family, friends, food to eat, books to read, and plenty of space to run and play.

My mother was the center of my world. I never wanted to leave her side. In the Midwest we'd have thunderstorms in the spring and on humid late-summer afternoons. The sky would suddenly get heavy and thick, the heat would start to weigh down on you, and just when you were getting tired from a day of running around in the field, the clouds would open up and rain would come down in sheets, the sky on fire with sudden lightning, the earth rumbling with thunder. This terrified me. When I was in preschool, it was the most frightening thing I could think of. And being with my mom was the only safe place. I'd run to her, hoping she would protect me. If the thunderstorm happened at night, I would try to get in bed with her. I didn't care if my brother or anyone else made fun of me—that was the safest place I knew. I've been in a lot of places in my life, and I've seen a lot of things, felt a lot of things. But I still remember being a little kid and being absolutely terrified by thunder until my mother let me know it was going to be OK.

My mother, Linda Shanklin, was hardworking, loving, and fierce. We never doubted that she cared for us, but we also knew that it was not wise to cross her. For one thing, she was six feet tall. I loved her a lot, but that didn't mean I wasn't scared of her. She had played basketball in high school and still had an athletic build and reflexes quick enough to snatch you up if you had the nerve to try something slick. For another thing, she knew that raising two black boys in a town like Springfield meant that they had to know exactly how to behave at all times. If she didn't get us in line and keep us in line, it could literally be the difference between life and death. The black section of Springfield was not an economically strong place. Unemployment was high, jobs were scarce, and people struggled. And when crack came, it just obliterated a lot of whatever safety and organization there was in the black community. On top of that, you had to worry about white police officers who were known for acting as judge, jury, and sometimes executioner in the streets. We rarely saw police officers as sources of protection or safety. At best, they were the last resort when you had absolutely no other choice. But for most of us, they felt more like another criminal element that you had to be careful of.

My mother knew that the options for black boys to end up imprisoned, hospitalized, or in a casket were many, and that the ways out were few. She knew really of only one way, and it was education and discipline. And she taught me these lessons with her own two hands.

One day in kindergarten, we were doing this cool little project where we all got red helium balloons. The idea was that we would write notes on them and let them go, and wherever they landed, someone would find our notes and write to our school. Pretty neat. So there we were, a troop of kindergartners, all marching out to the schoolyard with our red balloons all bouncing in the air on the end of long strings. We were supposed to wait for our teacher's word to let them go, but being the kid I was, I just couldn't do that. The temptation was too great. As soon as we got outside, I just let go of my balloon and watched it fly away into the sky. At first it was interesting, but pretty soon after, it hit me what I had done. I didn't have a balloon and everyone else did!

So I did what any little snot-nosed kid would have done. I walked over to a classmate and started telling him to let his balloon go too. Of course he didn't want to, so I just snatched it out of his little hand and sent it flying up to the heavens.

He didn't take that well. He started screaming and crying, which got the attention of our teacher and got me in trouble. When we got back to the classroom, she wrote my name on the board. A smarter kid would have just taken the loss and kept his mouth shut. But I was defensive. I've always hated being wrong, even when I know I am, so

I challenged her. "So what?" I said. "I didn't even do anything," which was obviously a lie.

This was way out of line, so she put a check mark next to my name for disrespect, which meant the situation was getting heated. Three checks meant you had to go to the principal's office. But in that moment I wasn't thinking the whole thing through. I was just mad that I'd let my balloon go, mad that I'd made this other kid cry, and mad that I'd gotten in trouble. And I wasn't going to back down. I've never liked the idea of people having power over me. Even if it's earned.

"So what?" I told her defiantly after the second check. "I don't care!"

Now the class was quiet. This was decidedly not the way you talk to a teacher in kindergarten, but I was unbothered. Nobody was going to push me around. Everyone is so used to doing whatever the grown-ups tell them, but it was dawning on me that they had no *real* power. I mean, so I go to the principal's office. Then what? He's just going to lecture me and tell me not to do what I'm doing. I literally don't care. I can keep saying no, and they can keep getting mad, but I'm still winning. This felt like a foolproof plan.

And it was. Right up until the moment Linda Shanklin walked into the principal's office while I was sitting there. They had called her to report on my misdeed, and she showed up as cool as a cucumber, calm and businesslike. She had to come in from work and was in her professional attire, which usually meant I was going to escape any kind of serious punishment. See, my mother had two modes. Weekend mode, when she didn't have makeup on, was when you had to be careful. She would get you as soon as you got out of line. She'd flash on you, pop you across the back of the head or whatever she needed to do to let you know she was in charge. You knew not to raise her attention then. But if she was in work clothes and makeup, you could always get away with just a little bit extra because that meant she had to deal with white people and the general public and there was pressure on her to be professional. My brother and I figured this out early, and we tried to use it to our advantage whenever we could.

She walked into the office and didn't even make eye contact with me. That's when I should have known something was about to go very wrong for me. Instead she turned to the principal and simply said, "You got something?"

Something like what? I wondered.

And that's when the paddle came out.

My mother beat my ass in the principal's office that day, and I will never, as long as I live, forget it. Disrespect, insubordination, acting out at *school?* Of all places?! This was everything she needed us not to do, and she was going to make that crystal clear.

When it was over, I cried. I cried all through the morning, cried all through lunch, all through story time and nap time. At recess I cried to my brother.

"Who did this to you?" he wanted to know. He was ready to fight someone. He and I didn't always get along, but no matter what was going on between us, both of us were always ready to protect each other from anyone else.

I could barely get it out. "Mommy did it!" I choked out through tears.

He just laughed. This was not something he could help me with.

That was the very last time I remember seriously acting up in school. Some kids get caught hundreds of times and still don't learn their lesson. I was different. You just had to tell me once. I had better things to do than to be in trouble all the time. It didn't make sense for me to bring home any issues with grades or behavior from school. I realized pretty quickly that if you pay attention, you can make things go smoothly for yourself. At least that's the way I saw it.

Pretty much everything I learned about how to be successful, how to show up for life, how to go for what I want, and how to be prepared came from my mom. She played high school basketball at Southeast, the high school I was supposed to go to. If she'd had the same opportunities that I had, her life might have turned out much differently. But there was really nowhere to go after high school for a female ball player in the 1980s. When I was coming up, we had the Amateur Athletic Union and tournaments and travel teams. We had coaches coming from all over the country and sneaker brands throwing money at our teams, making sure we had the best equipment, the best facilities, as we learned the game. If you're a boy and you had the talent, it could be developed. There was money behind it. Scouts would find you. Collegiate recruiters would show up at your games. Everyone knew that if you were good, they could make money from you.

My mom didn't have any of that. She met my dad, Frank Sr., who had come from Nigeria to work when he was about nineteen. He started off in New York City, then worked in Oklahoma and Texas before finally taking a job in Springfield with the Department of Children, Youth and Families. They fell in love, or something like that. One thing led to another and then here she was. Barely in her twenties in a small town with two boys to feed.

Still, my brother and I never went without. In fact you could argue that, at least among kids in our section of Springfield, we were almost spoiled. We always had the right clothes for every occasion. Church? We had suits. School? We had button-up shirts and clean, pressed pants. Winter? We had warm coats, hats, and scarves. And starting around sixth grade, I began to have basketball shoes. I remember my first pair of shoes that cost over one hundred dollars. Air Pennys in 1995. Blue and white. (This was before they introduced the Foamposites.) Going to school with those on, I legitimately thought I was about to levitate in the hallway. We were not, by any stretch, a wealthy family. We bought food in bulk from the discount grocery. We understood money to be something of great value—not to be wasted or taken for granted. But even when were at our most ungrateful, we still remembered that we were lucky to always have the lights on, to always have food in our home. We could see that not every kid around us had those things.

It wasn't until I was older, however, that I learned about the true sacrifices my mother had made for Frank and me to feel taken care of. One winter, when we were in elementary school, my mother's old car got stolen. Crack had hit Springfield sometime in the late 1980s, and by the '90s it was in full swing. Everything got stolen. Cars, radios, bikes, shoes, packages. If it wasn't nailed down, someone was going to take it. Obviously, buying a new car was not on the table. We were barely a paycheck away from having nothing. Fortunately, my mother's job at the Springfield Housing Authority was walking distance from where we lived, and so while not having a car was inconvenient, it was not enough to ruin us.

But then winter came. Temperatures were below freezing every day, often below zero with the windchill. My mother knew that she had to save money for a car, but Frank and I, two rapidly growing, athletic boys, needed coats. There wasn't enough money for all of us to have coats, so she made sure that we were bundled up and she went without. For an entire winter, she walked to work every day, and home every day, without a winter coat. She never complained to us about it. She never mentioned it. I don't even remember it happening. It wasn't until years later that my grandmother and later my stepfather told us the story. To this day, in fact, my mother has never told me herself that she spent an Illinois winter without a coat so that Frank and I could be warm. That's what I mean about Midwestern people. They get used to it. It is from her that I learned how to simply put my head down and work.

She cared a lot about manners and behavior, and she instilled that in us. I remember her always saying, "Don't embarrass me." If I could sum up almost all her guidance in once sentence, that would be it. We were to always say "please" and "thank you." We were to treat everyone in our community with respect. And don't let her find out that you were somewhere acting a fool out of the house. Springfield was a small town. We knew there were families that were wild and families that were respectable, and if Linda Shanklin had anything to say about it, we would be a family that was respectful.

But don't let that fool you. She had some street in her.

I remember once when I was in about sixth grade, she had been involved in a long interpersonal conflict with another woman in town. There was a whole history to it, and I'm not going to go into it all because I don't want to put anyone's business out there. But let's just say there was tension between these two women, words had been exchanged for a while, and tempers were hot.

One Saturday my brother and I were playing basketball down at the recreation center. My mother came to see our game, which she often did. Everything in Springfield was small enough that we could walk alone pretty much anywhere we needed to go, but whenever she could make it, Mom would come down to see us play. This particular day she happened to walk in and find herself, for the first time since the drama had started, face-to-face with this woman she had been beefing with for the past few months.

Linda Shanklin didn't say a word. There was no yelling, no

threatening, no chest bumping. She just took one look at her, cocked back, and busted this lady dead in the face. Next thing you knew, my mother was on top of her, beating her all the way down until people pulled them apart. This poor lady never stood a chance. It was so crazy to see that as a kid. On the one hand, no one wants to see their mom wilding out. But on the other hand, you kind of felt like, "Damn. My mom's a G." It kind of made me and Frank puff out our chests a little bit. It had been made known. We might be well behaved, but our family was nothing to be trifled with. This is how we learned to handle opposition where I grew up. Directly. Head-on. And quickly. I loved my mother. But I definitely had a very healthy fear of crossing her.

And yet we never, not even for a moment, doubted that she loved us. Not just loved us as children, but truly wanted the best for us. She cared for us, permanently and consistently, no matter how hard it was on her. She made the best of her life by focusing on doing little things, like her job, perfectly. Everyone around town seemed to know her. She worked at the Springfield Housing Authority as a development manager for twenty-two years and excelled at it. She was serious and professional, and she made sure that we were the same, that we read and did well in school and knew how to take responsibility for our-selves. At a young age, maybe when I was in third or fourth grade, I was doing my own chores, ironing my own clothes. Every Sunday I would take out my whole array of outfits for the week. I'd line them up. Iron each one. Make sure the creases were perfect, the collars pressed. It was important to me. I wanted to be good because Linda Shanklin wanted me to be good.

This was, for as long as I can remember, an integral part of how I viewed myself and the world. I just wanted to be good. I didn't want anyone to be able to say to me that they were better than me. Not at school, not at sports. Not even at picking out and ironing clothes. You might call it an obsession, or maybe something nonsensical, but it was important to me. It drove me in ways subtle and not so subtle.

With so many kids around, it was inevitable that we would play the dozens. Some people know of it as "your mama" jokes. As in, "Your mama so ugly she threw a boomerang and it refused to come back." For us, it was like verbal slap-boxing—you sharpen your wit, toughen your skin, and it's fun to watch. By the time we got around to it, mama jokes were kind of passé. Plus, we were all family, so how could you roast your cousin's mother if she's your aunt? Really, what we got into was critical roasts about how a person was dressed, their haircut, their shoes, anything. "Boy, your teeth so nasty three out of four dentists recommend suicide." It was always funny, but it could get painful real quick. That was the best part about it. It was like watching a balancing act between what was funny and what was cruel. When someone else was getting roasted, it was funny. When you were getting roasted, it was cruel.

I was one of the youngest kids around, so while everyone else was cracking jokes, I always felt a step behind. I tried to keep up, but I couldn't. My cousins were more practiced, more lightning-fast in their delivery. Everyone could say something to make the whole crowd bust up. I felt like I understood it but couldn't do it. It was like watching people fluently speak a language that you're just learning. And the worst would be when the attention finally turned to me, little Andre trying to lay low in the corner.

"But what about Andre ears though?" someone would say.

Damn.

It was all over after that. I got roasted for my ears, and I got roasted for being tall, and sometimes I got roasted for being the young one, but I could never come back. I was just not built like that.

That competitive streak, however, that part of me that wanted to be the best at everything, wouldn't let me get past that. On the outside I would just kind of quietly take it, laughing along. ("Yes, my ears *are* so big I could hear this joke before you made it. Ha-ha, very funny, cuzzo.") But inside I'd be like the count of Monte Cristo, keeping score of every person laughing, and plotting my revenge. I'd wait, patiently, for my opportunity to get back at them. Sometimes it would be trying to take everybody out in one of our family's frequent competitive Uno tournaments. (To this day, there still is no feeling sweeter than dropping a Wild Draw Four on some older cousin who's been roasting your haircut for three days.) But more often, it was sports. Something else just happened to me when we got to anything that involved running or quickness or athleticism. I suddenly felt like I was in charge. Even if older or bigger kids could beat me for now, I always knew that it was just a matter of time before I would catch up.

Springfield was great because you could always find organized sports to play, no matter how poor you were. Soccer, baseball, football, basketball. They went on all year round at the Boys & Girls Club, and pretty much everybody could afford it. The club was staffed by a bunch of older guys who, while I wouldn't exactly call them role models, were at least there consistently. You could always go down there after school or on a Saturday and there'd be the same dudes, usually in their late teens and early twenties, organizing games and showing kids the fundamentals of the sport. Sure, some of these guys were characters and hustlers and were almost definitely involved in some stuff out in the streets. But for the most part, all that noise got left outside when they got to the Boys & Girls Club. They were just there for us, and no matter what they did elsewhere, we looked up to them. Those guys were my first coaches, the first men whose standards for playing I tried to live up to. My brother, Frank, is working now to become a referee, maybe even in the NBA, and I have no doubt that this is because both of us were so heavily and positively influenced by city-run sports programs.

I started playing in little rec league games when I was about eight or nine years old. And I was already good enough to play on Frank's team, even though he was supposed to be two age groups above me. But that kind of thing fueled me. I needed to show him up in everything. If he had a candy bar, I'd want two. If he got a certain score in a video game, I needed to double it. And the competition went both ways. When kids would pick teams, we'd always make sure we never played on the same team. We had to go against each other. It was always like the game within the game. Off the field or court, our relationship wasn't combative, but it wasn't warm either. We were always on edge with each other. We rarely fought for real, but we'd play-fight daily—sneak up to try to catch each other off guard with a quick slap. I loved these kinds of competitions because mostly I could hold my own.

But things came just as easily to my brother as they did to me. He was at least as athletic as I was, and definitely a better football player. I believe that he could have played in the NFL if he really wanted to. I don't honestly think I ever surpassed him in terms of natural talent, speed, or strength. He was, in a lot of ways, too smart for his own good. He recognized from an early age that he could pass classes, graduate from school, and basically just float along without ever having to do any real work. I remember arguing about this with him in middle school. "Look," he said, "why would I bust my ass to get As when I can get Cs and still graduate the same as you with the same diploma? It just doesn't make any sense." We saw things so differently at the time, but it's hard for me to put into words how much I grew to appreciate him. Even when I look back on him he had a method to his madness. A lot of times I thought he was snubbing me because he didn't want to hang out with me. I would later learn that he didn't want me to get caught up in bad decisions he was making. When we were older and I was struggling with difficult times in my high school and college careers, he was one of the few people I always knew had my back. And even in high school when we went to rival schools, he would be cheering for me so loud from the stands that his friends would be looking at him crazy. No matter what was going on, I now realize that Frank always had my back.

When he put it that way about grades, he kind of had a point. But I just couldn't get with that strategy. For me, the point wasn't to get it done. The point was to get it done *better than everyone else.* I didn't want to be distracted. I didn't want to mess around and party and get caught up in social things. All I wanted to do was be good and beat everyone. And so almost everything I did revolved around that.

Those early days in Springfield shaped almost every single part of what makes me who I am. My grandmother taught me about responsibility and respect. My brother taught me competition and aggression, to never let anyone back you down. My rec league coaches taught me how to show up and how to put everything aside to attend to the kids who need you. And my mother. My mother taught me stoicism. Toughness. She taught me love and tenderness. She taught me sacrifice and discipline, and most importantly, she taught me to get the very best out of myself.

But there was another lesson. There would be times when I would just sit and watch her as she moved through the house, doing dishes or putting away laundry. Maybe she couldn't even tell my eyes were on her. And I would think about her life. A single mother living in her mother's attic with two unruly boys. Sacrificing and working an office job and keeping us fed and clothed. And I would look at Springfield as a whole. Our town was full of stories like that, of people who had, through some combination of fate and inertia, ended up with lives they didn't quite choose or wouldn't have chosen. It was a small place. And once you know the place you're in is a small place, the next most obvious question is what is the rest of the world like, and why are we all staying here? How can everyone be satisfied with a life built entirely around these long streets with low-slung clapboard houses and empty fields? How can everyone be OK with seeing the same people at the same grocery stores, the same bars, involved in the same drama, in the same streets, doing the same things every day? For some people, I guess that's fine. They want or need nothing more and they're happy. And that's great! But what about those of us who wanted more and could not have it? That's what really gave me the chills when I thought about it: the idea that you could really *want* to get out of this town and go into the whole world, and that you somehow still might not make it.

That's why my mother made us read the newspaper. She wanted us to know there was more. That's why she was so ruthless about teaching us work and focus, and communication, and respect. Because she knew that it would take every single drop of effort and sweat, every single good break and perfect behavior, every single paragraph read, and trophy won, and A+ earned, and letter of recommendation written for us to make it out of here and into that world. And even then, it might still be out of our hands.

"Springfield is a place," she told me once, "that if you're not careful, you can get stuck here." I didn't ask her what she meant by that.

I didn't have to. I could just look in her eyes and tell. I love where I grew up. And I love what it gave me. But something deep inside me would whisper at night, "If you don't do everything you possibly can, you'll be stuck here for the rest of your life." And I knew, from a very early age, that I just could not live with that.

02

Confidence

L ike life, basketball is a beautiful and complicated game. A game
with choreography and wrinkles, and endless motion and adjust-
ments. It's a game of instinct and telepathy and kinesthesia. It's a
game in which five people begin to think as one person, and
human beings sense and react to each other's movements even seconds before they are made. When it's played at its best level, it's a
ten-person magic show where we wow the spectators with feats that
defy explanation, no-look passes, shots made from impossible angles.
At its best, it's a game of alchemy.

But it's also a brutal game. A game of pounding joints and crush-
ing bones, ligaments ripped and healed crooked, noses broken, joints
dislocated. It happens fast and without apology, and once you step
onto the floor of a real game, it does not wait for you. Either you run
it or you get run over by it. That's why ultimately basketball is a

game of personal mettle and nerve. You have to decide every moment that you are on a court that you have every right to be there and every right to make decisions there. More than anything, basketball is a game of confidence.

There are good players and great players, but the technical distance between the best player in the NBA and the worst player in the NBA is really not that big. Everyone can shoot, everyone can dribble, everyone can pass, and everyone is strong. So confidence is really the thing that makes the difference between winning and losing. When I look back at my career, I can see now that each milestone I hit wasn't so much a milestone of technical ability, though there were those. They were really milestones of personal belief. Which means that they were moments when I had to believe in myself despite the fact that someone else was committed to making sure I didn't.

On the first day of seventh grade I walked into my first-period classroom. We had been given our bell schedule the day before, and I was excited to sit down and get started on a new year. I had been playing basketball and baseball and was starting to be interested in clothes and girls. Seventh grade held a certain kind of promise. I was going to play on the team, I had a little rep around town as something of a baller. And to top it off, I had on some crisp new gear, had a fresh haircut, and was looking to make an impression. This would be a good year.

I knew something was off, because when I walked into the room, I noticed that all the other kids were white. My middle school was fairly diverse, at least as far as black and white students went. And up until that point, it always seemed that every class I was in was at least somewhere between 20 and 30 percent black.

Even though it was unusual for me to be in an all-white class, there was a simple explanation for it today. I had been placed in the honors track. I didn't yet think a lot about why it was that the honors track meant all white students except for me. It just seemed like that's the way it was. I was more serious than most of the people I knew and was growing up around. I had been raised that way. And in no small part because of my mother's discipline about reading, my grandmother's lessons about behavior, and all my personal drive to be the best that I could possibly be, I was one of the kids in school chosen for advanced education. This meant I would get to do advanced projects, have extra privileges, and just generally achieve at a high level. I was excited.

But when I walked into the room, the teacher stopped me almost immediately.

"I think you might be in the wrong classroom, dear," she said.

"Nope. Right one."

I still wasn't really aware of what was happening. Obviously, I had read my schedule and knew which classroom I was supposed to go to. That's just basic. Still, she seemed unconvinced.

"Are you sure?"

"Yes, I'm sure, ha-ha." This whole thing was silly. I was already headed for a seat, thinking this little interaction was over. But it wasn't for her. She followed behind me.

"Can you show me your schedule, hon?" she said. This time she seemed a little more forceful.

It was then that I started to understand.

I presented her the schedule I had crumpled in my hand.

She looked it over for a moment. "Ah. OK," she said quietly. "Take your seat then."

I sat down slowly, reality dawning on me. Did that just happen? Did I really get asked to show my papers? In my own school? I looked around. Only a few kids had noticed. The rest were too busy catching up on the first day, talking and laughing while we waited for the bell to ring. My skin was hot. My heart was beating fast. The bell rang. I sat quietly and opened my notebook.

Race was not something that I became aware of in a moment. It was something that built slowly in my understanding of the world. I didn't run around when I was three years old thinking, "I'm black!" None of us do. Everything in my world seemed normal. My friends, family, community—these were the regular people. Our lives unfolded in a normal way. We had our own society filled with all kinds of people. And we thought it represented the entire world. Some of us were kind, some were rougher. Some were honest, some were tricky. Some were quick-witted or emotionally intelligent, some were slow thinking or oblivious. All of us were black. It didn't seem that our lives were organized around white people, or what they thought of us or could do to us. If I had any consciousness of white people, it was simply that they were somewhere else. They were "over there."

But as I grew, that changed, slowly but certainly. The freedom to be unaware of racism simply doesn't last long if you're black.

For one thing, my mother was not shy to bring it up. It was an important part of how she prepared us for the world and kept us safe. When we were growing up, it became clear that much of her guidance about behavior, respect, and self-control was really about how to steer clear of police officers, who, she knew, could be incredibly racist and harmful in the Midwest. It's funny to see in the past few years what many Americans are referring to as a sudden jump in racially motivated police brutality. But growing up in the 1980s and '90s, we took this for granted as a fact of life. Police may help you, but they may also hurt you. And the way you behaved didn't really have a lot to do with it. Good kids could catch a police beatdown just as quickly as the bad kids could. The best strategy was to steer clear of them altogether, because you just never knew.

We were raised to be respectful in general because my mother calculated that this attitude, if we held it deeply enough, could keep us out of the line of sight of law enforcement. But the struggle most of us face as black people is that respect gets you only so far. There are just as many times in which you have to be aggressive and fear- less, in which you have to not back down or cower in the face of people who would like to keep you in check. I've told you how my mother would get if you pressed her. Well, part of that is that black women have to be that way, otherwise people are always going to be pressing them. America is always going to be pressing you.

My grandmother represented a somewhat earlier version of this balance. She was one of the few people in those early years of my life who seemed to interact regularly with white people. She would often take me with her to pick up vegetables from local farmers, who were almost always white. As an avid food gardener herself, she empha- sized farm-to-table before that was even a thing. So oftentimes you could find her chatting it up with some white dude with rough hands and a dirty flannel shirt, talking about the soil this year or which way the weather would be coming in from. She was a woman from the South and of an older generation, so she was capable of getting along with everybody. Southern women of that age have a certain kind of magic with that. They can crack a joke and fix you with a smile that makes everything feel peaceful and easy.

But the truth about both of these women was that they would not hesitate to lay down the law with quickness and authority if you stepped out of line. They knew that they had to.

So I grew up learning a balance. On the one hand, it was "Yes, ma'am. No, sir." On the other hand, it was a deep sense that you simply couldn't let people fuck with you.

It seems to me, as a black man, that the rest of the world has a very hard time making sense of you if you have both these qualities in equal measure. When a black man is wild and unbridled, cursing every other word and breaking all the rules, then in an odd way the world is comfortable with that. They may complain about him, but they can write him off as a product of "the ghetto." They see him as uneducated, unfit to play by the rules they've set, to deal with the world they've created. He may be threatening to some minor extent, but if he gets too far out of line, there's a whole prison system designed to contain him. As a criminal, he represents no real systemic menace because he fits well within the expectations of white America. They can write him off. "Sure, he's talented," they may say, "but he's too street to ever have any real power."

Conversely, when a black man is respectable and buttoned up, when he speaks the language of white America with ease, when he blends in too well, never challenging, never threatening, then he buys himself a (very provisional) pass into whiteness. He goes to the right kind of school and holds the right kind of views, and white America embraces him with open arms because he, too, is not a threat. They know, albeit perhaps subconsciously, that his life (and privileges) are conditional, held in place by a tenuous social contract. His life is based on their acceptance. And he would be unwilling to risk that by deeply, publicly, and unapologetically challenging whiteness.

Both these ways of being in the white world are easily understood and, I think, represent a kind of comfort for many white people. But for structural racism, trouble comes in the form of a third kind of black person: the one who knows who they are and where they come from, who is unafraid to challenge the status quo and say things that make everyone's inner racist a little uncomfortable, but who also has their shit together, who is well read and well informed, who is unlikely to be squirreled away in a prison or rendered voiceless behind walls of poverty, who cannot be written off as uneducated or "thugged out." This, in my experience, is the kind of black person who represents the greatest threat to oppressive systems. At least it seems that way. Because I've learned that if you are in this third category, a lot of white people don't know what to make of you. And for the sake of their comfort, they pressure you, and hard, to be either one or the other.

This is not all stuff I had fully realized that morning in seventh grade. The consciousness was beginning, but it was not even close to having been formed. That morning in that classroom, being asked to, essentially, show my papers activated only one impulse in me: competition. If someone doubted me, then I would prove them wrong. That day, that teacher doubted me in a most fundamental way. She doubted my right to even *be* in the room. So that teacher and that idea—the idea that I don't even have a right to be in that room—is what I would spend the rest of my life proving wrong. And in small ways and in big ways, whether I wanted it to or not, race would be a silent but powerful guiding force that exerted its pressure on every step for the rest of my journey.

In a certain sense, it began before I was born, with a mother who knew that the two boys she loved had to earn extra levels of achievement just to stay safe and alive. And with a grandmother who grew up knowing about lynching, about the deep cruelty that could come from racism, and therefore learned how to get along with everyone, how to keep the ugliness at bay. They raised us with that. It was in our lives, every word was laced with it, and maybe in a sense it was even in our genetics. But for me, in another sense, it began in that moment in seventh grade when I learned that just standing in a certain room, complete and unafraid, was enough to make certain people uncomfortable. I didn't take it personally. I didn't internalize it or take is as subtle but inescapable proof that I was less than. How could I when I was raised by a mother who would sock a person in the face without a word just as quickly as she would go an entire winter without a coat to make sure her boys stayed warm? When you're taught this kind of confidence, you know better than to take some random woman's racism personally. Instead, I took it as a challenge.

You have to take it as a challenge. The alternative is too dark and too scary. This country is designed to wreak absolute havoc on the confidence of black people. You grow up learning over and over again about how people like you have been murdered and enslaved, and how they continue to be. You want to tell yourself that it's over and that that's not going to happen to you. But there are little moments all day long that come out of nowhere and remind you that you're not in charge and that the people in charge don't like you, and so you can never be 100 percent safe. Like a teacher looking at you not as if you are a student but as if you are a problem. Just because you happen to have good-enough grades to be in her class. And if you stop to think about that too much, if you let that feeling start to settle into your blood and bones, it's hard to recover from. You have to learn confidence. You have to own it. Or else you won't survive.

━━━━

One of the earliest and most important basketball influences in my life was Coach Lawrence Thomas. A short, dark-skinned man with a serious demeanor and large, sensitive eyes, he was both my very first Boys & Girls Club coach and an assistant coach of my junior varsity team at Lanphier High School. Coach Thomas has devoted his life to training young men to be basketball players. Which is to say he trains us to be disciplined and courageous. He's still coaching to this day, and I have had the opportunity to mentor and work with his son, bringing it full circle. But my earliest memories of him go back to when I was about eight years old. We were all scared of him because he seemed like someone who didn't have a lot of patience for fooling around. But the more we got to know him, the more he became like a father figure to all of us. He knew all our parents, waved to everyone around town. He was like the little mayor of black Springfield. He wasn't perfect, but he had integrity and respect.

He used to gas me up when I was in the third grade. "This kid gonna be in the NBA!" he would say when I was running down the floor just trying to keep the ball from slipping out of my control. I tried to pretend like that kind of stuff didn't matter. But every time he said it, I had to work to keep the smile from spreading across my face.

Everything Coach Thomas said carried some weight because he was tight with Kevin Gamble. Gamble was a legend to us. A six-foot-five guard out of Lanphier High School, Kevin was on those Celtics teams with Bird, McHale, and Dennis Johnson. Gamble's NBA career started when he was called out of the Canadian League after Bird was injured in November 1988. He ended up dropping 31 in the final game of that season. He went on to play ten years in the league in almost 650 games, averaging 9.5 points per game on 50 percent shooting. As far as we were concerned, this was fairy-tale stuff. Hearing a guy who coached Gamble telling me that I was going to play in the league was quite the boost! Stuff like that made me want to work harder. I still didn't believe that I was going to go to the league, but when a coach has your respect and supports you, you kind of don't want to disappoint him.

In middle school, Coach Brewer was another important person in developing my confidence. He was maybe the second person outside my family who treated me like he saw real, genuine potential in me. I first met him in seventh grade, and honestly I didn't think he liked me. He was not rough, per se, but businesslike. And he was funny. He would gently roast kids and make everyone crack up. He didn't act like basketball was serious. I think he knew that most of us just liked running around and pretending to be Jordan, and for the most part he was fine with that. He was realistic about what it meant to coach middle school basketball. He just wanted us to learn some basics of how to play and defend—and mostly to stay out of trouble. A thing I noticed about Coach Brewer was that he really seemed to like us. A lot of middle school teachers come off as if they're tolerating the kids. But Coach Brewer seemed to actually enjoy our enthusiasm and playfulness. He didn't make you feel like you had to be someone other than who you were, and I appreciated that.

Still, I don't think I caught Brewer's attention until the first report period was done and I got straight As on my report card. I'm not sure, but I might have been the only kid on the team who did that. I remember him coming up to me in the hallway soon after.

"Your grades. They're good!" He seemed almost surprised.

"Yes, thanks, Coach."

"Yeah, well . . . keep it up."

It was a small exchange, but it felt important because things changed noticeably between me and him after that. He was a little harder on me in practice but also more generous with his time. It was like he was suddenly taking me seriously. We would work extra drills together, and I started to make a habit of hanging around his office after school even on days when we didn't have practice. Sometimes he and I would just sit on the bleachers and talk about everything in the world except basketball. School, girls, politics, growing up. It wasn't what we talked about that mattered so much. It was the fact that we talked at all. That was really the difference.

See, any kind of greatness takes work. Everyone knows that. But what fewer people understand is that work itself takes faith. You have to have faith that the work you're doing will bring about results, otherwise you'll lose interest. Coaches like Brewer and Thomas made sure that I saw a direct relationship between my work and the results. That's what their encouragement was. The fact that Coach Brewer took a moment to notice my grades and started treating me differently afterward, started investing time in me, made me feel like my work had value. The fact that Coach Thomas always had a kind word for me, always told me that he believed in me, made me feel like I was doing something right. That's what I had a hard time explaining to my brother. It was true that you didn't have to work to graduate or get by. But you had to work to see results. That was my theory, at least. But Coaches Brewer and Thomas made sure that theory was proven true.

Seventh grade turned into eighth grade and life threw me a wicked curveball. Up until that point, I had gotten pretty used to being one of the best basketball players on the floor. I knew how to at least pretend to be humble, but secretly I thought that most of my success had to do with my talent, my hard work, and my skills. And to an extent it did. But what I didn't account for was how great a percentage of my early basketball success came from the simple fact that I was taller than everyone else. Turns out that accounted for a lot of it. And the way I found out was that the summer before eighth grade, pretty much every kid on every team we played had had a growth spurt except me.

I noticed it right away even in scrimmages. Shots I used to be able to get off with ease were now being blocked. My passes were picked off, and I was turning the ball over left and right. The way you see the court accounts for everything you're able to do out there, and just the few inches' difference between how the court looked in seventh grade and how it looked in eighth grade completely changed my ability to play the game. What used to be a wide-open field with an endless horizon was now a forest overpopulated with tall bodies and sweaty, waving arms. It messed with my confidence. As the year wore on, my sense of myself as an exceptional athlete slowly faded away. Maybe I had never been that good. Maybe it really was just that I was tall.

This started to change everything about who I was. My grades began to slip from As and Bs. I was doubting my purpose and losing clarity about where I fit into the scheme of things. It wasn't that I stopped working on the court. It's that the work seemed like it wasn't generating the returns that I was used to seeing. Coach Brewer still had me playing point guard and acting as the de facto leader of the team, but without the ability to score at will, I had to start looking for other ways to contribute.

In some sense that eighth-grade year was a blessing in disguise. I began to take my first step back from the game. Let's see, I thought. You have four other guys on the court. Each of them can do at least one thing pretty well. I started watching the other players more closely. I would notice that a particular kid who maybe wasn't that athletic was nonetheless good at setting screens, and Coach Brewer had taught me that screens didn't have to be used only to get the ball handler open. They could also be used to free up a shooter. Now that I was less inclined to make my own shot all the time, I started seeing the movement on the floor from a different perspective: This guy likes to stay in the corners, and if I can find him when he's open, he can maybe knock down a shot. This guy is just learning how to cut. If I can get the ball to him in motion, we can penetrate the defense and make a play. There were moments that season when it almost felt like the game was happening in slower motion. Once my focus was off my defender and how I could beat him, it was like a whole other layer of basketball opened up to me.

As the year went on, I started to gain a little bit of my confidence back. I still didn't like the fact that I was no longer the tallest kid on the floor, but I had somewhat gotten used to it by figuring out how to develop other skills. But the biggest thing about the second half of the eighth-grade year was that you had to choose a high school.

Springfield has two public high schools to pay attention to as far as sports are concerned: Southeast and Lanphier. (Sorry, Springfield High.) And to put it bluntly, Southeast was the black school and Lanphier was the white one. Everyone from my neighborhood, everyone from Franklin Middle school, where I went, was supposed to go to Southeast. It was more than a neighborhood thing. It was a family thing. My mother had played for Southeast back in the early 1980s. My uncle Sam Fields did football and wrestling there and even went on to coach there in his later years. My brother went to Southeast. That was just what my family did.

I understood all that. But the thing about Lanphier was that was where all the good players went, all the guys I used to read about in the newspaper. Jeff Walker, Leonard Walker (Jeff's cousin), Victor Chukwudebe—all these guys would go on to Division I schools, and all of them were playing for Lanphier when I was in middle school. I was starting to pay closer attention to these things. I didn't yet have a real expectation of going pro, but I was serious about basketball and team rankings, and it was clear that Lanphier was the place to be.

And they were recruiting me—at least, one Lanphier coach was. His name was Pat McGuire. We used to call him Juice. He knew about me because I had gone to all the Lanphier summer basketball camps every year from like third grade to eighth grade. And the whole time, he and all his coaches were pumping me up. "You're going to be the next one," they'd say. "We need you at Lanphier." After an eighth-grade year spent struggling and feeling closer to average than I had ever felt, this was music to my ears. I wanted to go where I was wanted. And even though Lanphier wasn't my community, it was the school, in my mind, you had to go to if you wanted to be great.

It was a hard choice, a choice between who people wanted me to be and who I wanted to be. I was *supposed* to bring pride to Southeast, which had always felt like something of an underdog in Springfield sports. The rivalry between the two schools was not a rivalry at all. Lanphier beat Southeast in almost every sport almost every time. Lanphier had won a state championship. Southeast had never come close. Lanphier had Kevin Gamble and Ed Horton, who had played in the league, not to mention having a ton of Division I college players. Southeast had nothing like that. In some ways it was the classic Springfield dilemma. Do you stay where you are because it's what everyone else is doing? Or do you go away, disappoint some people you love, and shoot for something bigger?

It was a hard choice but a clear one. Still, there were people who had trouble with my decision. As word started to spread about the fact that I was bailing on Southeast to go across town, I noticed what I thought might be animosity. Kids would make comments that sounded like jokes but had a little bit of an edge to them. People didn't hang out with me as much after school, not even my teammates, and my social circle narrowed. I found myself spending more and more time alone during that eighth-grade year. I don't know if it was jealousy or just straight-up adolescent awkwardness, but everything felt out of whack.

One day I was walking down the hallway after school, probably headed to the gym to get some shots in before practice started. I passed one of the middle school assistant coaches, a white guy. He and I didn't have much of a relationship, but we certainly knew each other. Something about him had always rubbed me the wrong way. I tried to nod a quick hello and keep going, but he stopped me.

"Andre," he said. "Heard you're going to Lanphier." It wasn't a question but a statement.

"Yes," I replied.

"That's cool," he said. "You'll probably end up a loser just like the rest of those guys."

Everything inside me stopped. It was hard for me to believe what I had just heard.

I just mumbled, "Whatever, man," and kept it moving. I knew he was trying to get to me, and I didn't want to give him the satisfaction. But it angered me. It seemed so wrong for an adult to be actually rooting for you to lose. Walking down the hallway, I could feel his words echoing in my head. Why did he think they were losers? Those high school players were heroes to me. I loved them even more than I did the players we watched on *NBA on NBC* every Saturday. That's how serious high school basketball is in Illinois. Professional players were cool, but they were at a distance. Anyone in Springfield could pay four dollars to watch the most exciting games in the state, and when Jeff Walker broke away at full speed and got a dunk that was frozen forever in time on the sports page of the *Journal-Register*, that was the most amazing thing I could think of. Why couldn't he see that? Why did he think I was going to be a loser? None of it made sense.

I kept turning the conversation over in my head, rewinding and replaying the exchange like a song on tape. And the more I thought about it, the more I began to feel like something must be wrong with *him*. Not with me or with Jeff Walker. This was a coach I instinctively never liked anyway, and now I just had confirmation of my feelings. He was an asshole. Plain and simple. Like a lot of white people in Springfield, he didn't like us. It didn't matter what we did. We were always going to be losers in his mind. He may have been an adult, but I realized there was absolutely no reason to respect him.

You can't have respect for people who haven't earned it. That's pretty much the number one way to *become* a loser. This world is full of people who demand that you live by their rules and try to hate you for not doing that, even though there's literally nothing in their lives proving that what they're doing works. It's crazy. And if you're not discerning, if you're not careful with who you take seriously, and who you dismiss, then you'll spend a lifetime running in circles, trying to please and emulate the wrong people and getting nowhere. I knew I was trying to get somewhere, so some loser assistant coach for sure wasn't going to stand in my way. Fuck that guy. Now I was *definitely* going to Lanphier. And I was going to win there too.

━━━

I started at point guard freshman year. I was five foot ten already, so I was pretty big to be playing point. But there was a kid on our team, Tony Smith, who was six-one and could play all the positions. He had already hit his growth spurt. I would learn about that soon. But I accepted it. I trusted Coach Thomas and felt that if he thought I had things to learn before being a starter, then I had things to learn.

I started knowing how to read defenses and figure out what people's tendencies were on the floor. I watched how Tony directed traffic and set guys up for shots, feeding them at the perfect spot for them to do their thing.

When I wasn't playing basketball, I was on the track team. I'd always had a natural athleticism, but now there was coaching to go along with that. I started to understand my body more and learn which kinds of workouts helped me and which didn't. I saw that I had a long way to go to increase my speed, agility, and endurance. I competed in the triple jump, but my favorite thing was the high jump. I was fascinated by the precision and achievement of it. It was not subjective, like basketball. It was precise and measured. In track and field you could see your progress with numbers. You could set a target and beat it and then set another one. There was no gray area in track, and I liked that.

The summer after freshman year, Pat "Juice" McGuire was already coach of the JV team and pretty much came for me right away. He took me on as a kind of project, grooming me to take over the team. I spent much of that summer in the high school gym, working out with Juice and shooting drills. Even though freshman year had been good for my court vision and basketball IQ, my shot was still inconsistent. I had developed this inconsistent release, where sometimes my release point was way up above my head and the next time it'd be down by my chin. It was never the same. Juice kept me in the gym that summer sharpening things up, and I began to feel like I had a purpose again. I would wake up in the morning just loving the fact that I was going to be thinking about basketball all day. I'd have a quick breakfast, maybe play *Madden* or *NBA Live* solo around 5:00 am.

It would already be humid, and I'd get a good sweat on just getting to the facility. Kids would yell out to me as I passed by, ask if I wanted to hoop with them. But I didn't have time for it. I had something bigger going on. It was my first experience of feeling like a professional, and I loved it. Basketball had become big enough in my life that there were gradations. What you played at the park, that was casual. What you did on a team, that was academic. But those long afternoons spent in the gym, that felt professional. I was a craftsman. I had a craft. My whole days were spent in a laboratory going deep into the minutiae of the game with Juice cheering me on. He used to call me "Franchise." "Good shot, Franchise." "Pick it up, Franchise. Move your feet. Arms up, arms up, Franchise!" That made me laugh.

He also let me go along with the varsity team on summer tournaments. I couldn't get enough basketball. This was the academic part. The film study, if you will. I was picking up on little subtleties of the game. I could see the mistakes other coaches were making in their defensive schemes, the way guys would go under a screen when they should have gone over top. I started to notice that there's really a rhythm to each game, a flow over the progression of the contest that has everything to do with how coaches sub guys in and out, how the bench works, and who can make a final push in a close game.

With the exception of a little job I had reracking magazines at the library, I spent that entire summer in gyms. Either watching seniors play or working out with Juice, who kept telling me, "Franchise, next year is gonna be our year, Franchise. We're going to do it next year." I think he appreciated having me around as much as I appreciated being around him.

When I walked into school the first day of my sophomore year, a teacher stopped me again. But this time it was for a whole different reason. It was Coach Patton, the coach of the varsity team.

"Andre?" he said, looking me up and down.

"Yes? What?"

"Oh my god—come over here!"

He took me into his classroom (he was also the chemistry teacher) and led me over to a ruler he had on the wall.

"Stand against that." I did.

"You're six-four!"

Oh. This explained why everyone was staring at me in the hallway. I had somehow managed to grow five full inches over the summer. I mean, I knew I was growing. My pants were fitting weird, and at one point that summer I had just barely dunked (my first ever dunk), which felt pretty cool. But I had no idea how serious it was until I saw the look on Coach Patton's face as he measured me against that wall.

"You need to come try out for varsity!" was pretty much the next thing out of his mouth.

So sophomore year saw me playing on both the varsity and the JV teams at the same time. But it didn't really get to my head. First of all, I barely saw the court on varsity. Maybe if it was garbage time and we were up by, say, 20 points, I'd get in the game. But for the most part, I was a glorified equipment boy sitting at the end of the bench. The good part was that I got to practice and work out with those guys and the game continued to open itself up to me slowly.

The other reason it didn't get to my head was because playing varsity as a sophomore was nice, but the real flex was to play as a freshman. That's when you knew you were a legitimate threat. And on the team I played on, there was only one kid who did that: Rich McBride.

How can I describe my relationship with Rich McBride? He would become my closest friend during those high school years. Not necessarily because we were so naturally compatible but because we shared one thing in common: an absolute blinding obsession with the game. Rich and I worked out together, read stats together, followed high school rankings from all across the nation together. It seemed like all our time together was spent in a basement somewhere or at my grandmother's house talking about ball, watching ball, playing 2K. It was a meeting of like minds, and it made both of us better. There was no one else around us as deeply obsessive about the game as we were. Everybody else knew how to turn it off after a while. Rich, up until that point, was the only guy I ever met who was as driven as I was.

After we were on the court together for a while, it seemed that we could read each other's mind. I knew where he was going to be at all times. When I played point, I could almost feel him moving behind me. I could deliver the ball to a spot before he even got there. Sometimes before he even knew he was going there.

When Richie came to Lanphier, he was a big deal. Here's this six-foot-two freshman guard who's already on the varsity team. Dudes were going out of their way to dap him up. Girls followed him around the hallways like he was giving out candy.

Coach Patton set Rich up to be the starting point guard and basically built the team around him. In doing so, he had to sit a couple of seniors who had been playing for a while, and this was a move for which he caught a lot of flak. Even at the high school level, people in Illinois take basketball very seriously. Parents and other folks in the community were in no way psyched that kids were being forced to sit out their senior year to make room for a superstar freshman. But I can see now what Coach Patton was doing. He knew that team wasn't really going to win. They were going to sectionals, maybe, but Patton was thinking of it in the long term. He made Rich the focal point so he could prepare him to take over the team. And it made sense. Rich McBride was the future. That year national magazines had him ranked higher than almost any freshman in the country, including this one dude out of Akron, Ohio, named LeBron James.

That was when I started thinking about the strategy of basketball and about the business of it. Not just about how to build something for today but how to position a project for long-term success. And Rich was impressive to me because, for him, all that doubt went in one ear and out the other. He took the ball as a starting freshman and didn't back down.

The other thing I learned that year from Rich was about something called the AAU. I had never heard of it. When we hung out after school, I would hear him talking about some mythical travel team he played for based all the way in Chicago. What was that? How do you play for a team in Chicago when you're in Springfield? But here was this fourteen-year-old, traveling nationally, playing tournaments in far-flung places like Chicago and Indianapolis. Meanwhile I was still doing games with junior varsity and it was getting ridiculous. Dunking was now commonplace, and all the work I did with Coach over the summer was paying off handsomely. I was scoring like 25 to 30 points a game. It was a little bit of a Wilt Chamberlain situation.

I would always try to get my mom to come to my varsity games, but she wasn't having it. Often the JV and varsity games were back-to-back. I'd go from being the man in one game to warming the bench in the next one, and she couldn't stand that. "Why do we have to stay for the varsity games, Andre? You ain't playin'! You're just sitting there." *Mom.* "I'm not waiting around two hours just to watch you playing with a towel on the bench."

Playing on both teams created another complication. There was this rule in place that a kid could only play in three tournaments a year. But if you played on both teams, there were way more than three tournaments happening. You had the Freshman City Tournament, sophomore and junior tournaments. There were also Christmas and Thanksgiving tournaments. Altogether there could be as many as seven tournaments I was eligible for, which meant I had to make some tough choices.

I wasn't sure what to do. I wanted to play in the varsity tournaments because those are the bigger deal. But Juice, the JV coach, was my man. He'd been looking out for me since I was a kid. It was a tough situation. Do you play varsity, where you could get your name up and maybe get some scarce minutes in front of scouts, or do you stay loyal to the coach who was loyal to you?

One day I was talking to Lawrence Thomas about it, sort of complaining about how I wasn't getting varsity minutes because Coach Patton didn't think I was ready. Coach Thomas just looked at me.

"Andre, I've been telling Patton to put you on all year! It's Juice who keeps telling him you're not ready! You should play, man—you *been* ready. Juice just doesn't want you to start on varsity because he's afraid he might lose you on JV."

I couldn't believe it. My own coach had been holding me back so he could win. And it worked. We dominated. We lost only one game that year. But it really flipped the script for me. And it was not the last time this would happen. I would learn later that even at higher levels, coaches would lie to you and everyone else just to keep you where they needed you. That was when I started to see that just because a coach is nice to you doesn't mean you can trust them to have your best interests at heart. At the end of the day, they're only looking out for themselves. I never confronted him about that, but it taught me a new level of the game.

During that year our team was invited to what's called a shootout. It's not officially a tournament, but rather a one-game showcase for scouts to see who the talent was. Teams were assembled of the best players from different regions. At that point our main man was Rich, but Illinois had a whole crop of talent who would play in college and the pros. Darius Miles, a senior out of East St. Louis, was maybe the most-talked-about player in the country.

The point of the shootout was to showcase Rich McBride. But I was able to get a few minutes in the game. I was starting to understand that in games like this the main thing you wanted to do was not mess up on a big stage. Guard your man, grab rebounds, and try not to get beat too badly. My goals were modest. At the end of the game, we were early in an offensive possession. I had the ball, and while I was looking for someone to pass to, I realized that the lane in front of me was completely open. I guess the guy guarding me had gotten lost on a screen or something. I didn't have time to think about it. I saw an open lane right to the rim and I went for it. All that high-jump work must have added up, because when I dunked, the entire gym felt it. It's different to get a dunk in a high school game, because everyone there is a student and they're looking for any reason to get hyped. But this was a professional-type event. There were guys in the stands wearing suits. And when I completed that dunk and heard, even as I ran back on defense, the sound of people still buzzing and tittering, I knew that I had done something. It didn't feel like a big dunk to me, but it felt like a big dunk in the gym.

Afterward, I was walking through the tunnel and passed Darius Miles, whose game was long finished. "Yo, nice dunk," he said to me and kept on walking. I could barely believe it. *"That was Darius Miles! And he liked my dunk!!!"*

Our varsity team that year went to sectionals (equivalent to second round in NCAA tourney) and lost. We were in a playoff game against Quincy High, a team about 100 miles due west from Springfield. About a day before the game, we learned that our big man, six-foot-six Montez Slater, had hurt his wrist in a pickup game. This was terrible news. Here we were making a push for a state title, and all of a sudden we were without a center. Coach Patton had to reorder the lineup, which meant that I was no longer going to spend the entire game on the bench. I was going to see my first significant varsity minutes, and it was going to be on the biggest stage I had been on yet.

I tried not to be nervous, but I was. I kept reminding myself that this was what I'd been training for. I'd been good at every level, and Coach wouldn't put me in if he didn't think I was ready. To make matters worse, Quincy High was one of the most dominant programs in the country. It was ranked fourth in the nation in all-time high school victories and had not gone more than a few years without winning at least a regional title. Most of this had to do with the Douglas family, which was this insane collection of kids, nephews, and grandkids who all played basketball. There were like thirteen Douglases who played for Quincy over the years, including Bruce, who was the point guard on the 1981 national championship Quincy team and was named Mr. Basketball, and Dennis, who was an all-state forward. The one I had to guard in that game was Andy Douglas, a sharpshooter who already had like 100 threes in his high school career (which was a lot back then).

Coach put me in early, and all I was thinking about was going out there to compete. Nothing fancy. But as the game wore on, it stopped feeling like I was in a big game and was more like I was just doing what I knew how to do. I made some decent plays. I got a few steals and defended my man as well as I could. Mostly I was looking not to score, but to direct traffic and set other guys up. Quincy was a good team. Well coached and very smart. But it occurred to me that we were too. At least, we would be if I had anything to say about it. I felt like it was my job to learn Quincy for the team and to get everyone up to speed as quickly as I could. If I noticed a certain player always went to his left, I was going to share that. If I saw that they were defending our pick-and-roll a certain way, I wanted to make sure our guys knew what to expect. The crowd was incredibly loud, and we could barely hear ourselves think, but I felt like it was my job to keep everyone calm and playing the way we knew how to play.

Quincy was a better team than we were, and we lost that game. But it changed something in me. It was another point of proof that if you threw me into a situation, I knew enough about the game now to handle it. Maybe that was when I really started trusting myself. The very next day I went to a track meet and jumped six feet, six inches in the high jump. The previous year my highest mark was six feet, one inch. I don't know what had changed. It seemed like nothing. But it seemed like everything.

The following summer I played all the time in local high school summer leagues and tournaments. Two or three games a week. I was energized and confident. It was all coming together. Now I could catch lobs, posterize guys. It was a blur. But it was amazing.

Unlike me, who was still basically a high school kid, Rich Mc-Bride was operating his career like a mini professional. He was playing with a different AAU team now, and he had basketball connections seemingly all over the state. Plus, the University of Illinois had been recruiting him since he was, like, twelve, so he knew a bunch of players and coaches in that program. The two of us borrowed a car and drove up to Champaign-Urbana to scrimmage with some guys from the university. I didn't have any real plans or designs for my career out of this. I just thought it'd be cool to see how these guys play. The big name at Illinois basketball that year was Cory Bradford, a six-foot-three guard with a no-nonsense game who could score from anywhere. He was not flashy but he was nice. He could catch-and-shoot, pull up, get to the hole a little bit. He was the team's leading scorer with 494 points in his freshman year and led his team in three-pointers made each of the four years he played.

Somehow in this pickup game, that's the guy I ended up guarding. The Division I starter and leading scorer was going to be guarded by a high school junior. I was pretty much prepared to be toasted. My only hope was that he would maybe take it easy on me because I was a kid. But as the game went on, I kind of forgot who he was. Not disrespectfully, but because to me he seemed like just a good player. Not some kind of monster like he had been made out to be in my imagination. I really thought this was going to be child versus adult, but for the most part, I felt like I was guarding a regular player. I was even able to block a shot or two of his, which felt satisfying.

"This dude ain't *that* good," I said to Rich on the way home. "You know what I mean? I mean, he was nice, but the difference between him offensively and me defensively wasn't as big as I thought it would be." I would probably never have thought about that game or trip again except for the fact that when I came home, I found out that somehow it had been written up in the paper! To this day I don't know how it happened, but there it was: Andre Iguodala, Lanphier junior, locked up Cory Bradford in a scrimmage in Champaign. The fact that anyone cared surprised me even more than the fact that I held my own against a ranked Division I school's leading scorer. It was the first inkling I had that people were maybe going to start paying attention to what I was doing.

As silly as it seemed to me, that article changed things. My mom started to really see that this basketball thing was for real. My family began to see the big picture. They were much more willing to let me travel, put in extra time, and prioritize ball. And the timing couldn't have been better, because Rich had been talking to his AAU coaches about me. They had seen me at a tournament and knew who I was, and soon I was invited to play with them in New York City. Mostly these were Chicago kids, so I felt pretty much like a country bumpkin. I was wide-eyed. Now that I fly practically every week and have traveled a bunch, played in London and China, hooped with men from the state of Georgia to the eastern European country of Georgia, it doesn't seem like a big deal, but for all of us on that team, the difference between Chicago and Springfield might as well have been the difference between Earth and Mars. To those guys, I was very much the outsider. Awkward and remote, self-conscious and foreign. I wasn't up on the new slang, the new music that was happening for them. It was, to put it mildly, an uncomfortable process. They teased me the way any group of teenage boys from Chicago would tease a random kid from a small town. On top of that, this was a group of guys who all could hoop at a very high level. Some of these players were ranked top 10 nationwide. One guy went to Duke, another to Illinois. If I recall correctly, every player on that team eventually went to a Division I program.

But the best part was seeing top players from all over the country in the flesh. There's a scene in the movie *White Men Can't Jump* where they arrive at a tournament and they're sizing up all the competition. Well, this was exactly like that. Here were all the guys we had been reading about in magazines assembled in one place. Bracey Wright on the Texas squad. Dajuan Wagner, Kevin Tolbert. All these guys. I saw some white kid knocking down shots like he was buttering bread. I had never seen anything so smooth. "Who's that?" I asked. Turns out it was JJ Reddick.

And the competition was at an entirely new level. Guys were playing hard every single possession, and everything felt different. When you played a high school game, it felt like you were basically at home. Your mom and aunties and cousins would be in the crowd. Your teachers were there, as were your classmates. Of course you were trying to win and play hard, but the fact that you were in a high school gym with your whole community made everything a little softer. But here were all these kids from all over in New York City without their families. Everyone seemed so much older. Like we were a bunch of grizzled mercenaries. It was weird to see kids behaving like that, and it took some getting used to. They threw me in for like four to five minutes one game, and I got bumped, pushed around. Everything was just so much faster. At the beginning I was just trying to keep up. These guys weren't just playing basketball. They were fighting for scholarships. In a sense they were fighting for their lives. And many of them were bigger, older, and more experienced than I was. That first day, my motto was what it always was: just don't mess up.

But by the second day, something dawned on me. Thinking about how I had played the day before, I realized that I hadn't felt like myself. In the Quincy game there was a moment when I started to feel like myself. In the Illinois scrimmage, there was a moment when I started to feel like myself. What I mean is that there was a moment when my mind was completely on the game in front of me. Not on if I'm playing well, or if I'm good enough, or did Coach see that mistake. But simply on the game. But that wasn't happening here. So why? Was it because I was trying not to mess up? Because I felt like my normal game wouldn't be good enough for this court so I had to keep from playing my normal game? But was that right? I looked around the floor during warm-ups. The same kids were talking, shooting, stretching. But they no longer looked like mercenaries or little basketball soldiers. They looked like what they were—kids. With parents or grandmothers at home. Kids who really loved playing or were at least good enough at it that they had been flown out to New York City to do it. Which was the case with me. I had watched them all play yesterday, and there just wasn't anyone here I felt like I should be afraid of. I mean, there were probably kids who were better than me at certain things. But they were all here because they were good enough. And wasn't I here because I was good enough? So, I decided to tell myself that I belonged here. I don't care if this kid is a McDonald's All American. I don't care if that kid was in *Sports Illustrated*. I can hoop with these guys because I can hoop with anyone.

And as soon as the ball tipped off for our game, I felt, again, like myself. I don't even remember if we won or lost. I just know that I was no longer afraid.

That night me and a bunch of my teammates took a ferry to Times Square. It was early fall and the city was buzzing. We were drunk with excitement and with energy. I felt like there were a million lights in my body, just blinking and shining. I was young, I felt like a winner. It seemed the whole world was just there for us to take.

I took my little money that my mom had given me and bought myself a fake Rolex and some fake gold chains. I knew they weren't real, but I didn't care. They were beautiful. I took those things with me back to Springfield, clutching them to my chest like gold medals.

My senior year was a blur. I played, I studied, I worked. But everything was changing. Not just about basketball but about life. I had realized that there was a whole outside world and that I was going to go as far away as I possibly could. Basketball was transforming right in front of me. It was still a game, but it was becoming something else. A life. A dream. A business. A way forward. And soon, it would be a way to college.

03

When the Sun Is Too Hot

There are moments where something in us changes, something happens that determines the direction of our lives. Sometimes we know it plainly at the time. The night I was drafted, for one. Hearing my name called, ninth overall, I knew that all the times I stayed up late watching film, missed parties, got up early to run or lift, all the times I pushed myself far beyond my threshold of pain to get stronger or faster, were about to pay off handsomely.

But sometimes these moments are mundane and quiet. They are nothing special. You don't know what they mean until years later. Like this one, from when I was a kid. Just a sophomore in college. All the way out in Arizona.

I was standing awkwardly in the clubhouse of a luxury golf and country club. The room was packed with bodies. I was nineteen years old and sweating through my white polyester golf shirt. It had been

an entirely exhausting day. First I had to make small talk in the clubhouse with the gaggle of university boosters who showed up for this
event. I watched them downing drinks while I sipped on a soda water.
I stood awkwardly between them trying to look relaxed in my six-
foot-six frame while they joked about business deals and real estate
situations and a host of other things I didn't have any relationship to.
Occasionally I'd look across the room, hoping to make fleeting eye
contact with a teammate, another member of my Arizona Wildcats
basketball squad who'd been dragged out for these awkward booster
meet and greets. Maybe it would be Hassan Adams, the six-four
guard out of Inglewood who looked like he was faring no better over
by the bar, shifting awkwardly from one foot to the other, a forced
smile pasted on his face. Hassan was trapped too. A skinny white guy
with an alarmingly red face and a crown of hilariously perfect silver
hair was talking excitedly to Hassan, probably offering up an opinion
on how to best defend the UCLA backcourt or something. Hassan
was nodding earnestly with his forehead wrinkled up in an extreme
display of caring, like he was listening to the guy describing how his
wife died or something.

Meanwhile, in my conversation, a booster was asking me where I
was from.

"Oh. Um, Springfield, Illinois."

"Springfield! Birthplace of Lincoln!"

Birthplace of Lincoln. Every time someone asked me where I was
from, they would respond, "Birthplace of Lincoln!" as though that
had something to do with him. What in the hell was I supposed to say
to that? Yes, I was born in the same place as a guy who became president when I would have been a slave. Amazing coincidence, right?
That's something I thought about a lot actually: Why was it that
white people always mentioned that I was born in the same city as

Lincoln? I could never remember a black person bringing up a president who had been dead for almost 150 years right after asking me that question. Black people ask me different things. "What's it like there? Is it wild? Do you have siblings? Who do they listen to out there?" Questions that have to do with my actual life. Not some random factoid about a state. But this, I would learn, is small talk, a hilarious phrase if you think about it.

"Yes," I said, and let the awkward silence sit.

"That's a long ways from out here. What brings you all the way out to Arizona? Hoping to get a suntan?!"

This guy was firing on all cylinders. I looked over at Hassan again, hoping even harder to catch his eye, but SuperGramps was still talking, now gesturing wildly, telling a story he clearly thought was absolutely hilarious. Hassan was nodding with his eyebrows raised as if it was the craziest thing he'd ever heard in his life. He looked downright uncomfortable. I wondered if I looked that awkward. I didn't like that idea. I always prided myself on being better than most at dealing with white people. I was never intimidated, nor did I buy their particular brand of bullshit. I'll put it like this: If I were in the story "The Emperor's New Clothes," I'd be the kid who pointed out that it was all fake.

"No. Coach Olson has such a great program, such a storied tradition, that it made sense to come here and help us compete for a national championship."

Despite myself I was starting to talk like this a lot now. I guess in some way I was practicing for press conferences and interviews. It was how I had heard all the greats phrase things when talking to outsiders. Michael Jordan, Penny Hardaway, Jalen Rose, Scottie Pippen—all these guys had mastered a deep, dry, low-volume, and perfectly bland way of declining to reveal anything without actually being rude. I already had to practice it when I was being recruited senior year and reporters from the *State Journal-Register* called my house asking if I had signed a letter of intent yet. I had to practice it when I was interviewed by the campus paper and whenever I was approached at the grocery store by alumni who wanted to talk X's and O's with me.

I hoped the "storied program" answer would close the subject. I wasn't really trying to tell this guy the whole reason I came all the way to Arizona, the weirdest, whitest, hottest, driest, most western place a black kid from the Midwest could have gone. I wasn't trying to tell him about how I'd originally blown off Arizona's famous coach, Lute Olson, to sign a letter of intent with black Arkansas coach Nolan Richardson. I had decided that I only wanted to go to a program with a black coach because the racial dynamics of all black kids being yelled at by grown white men had always bothered me. Richardson had come to my house, sat in my living room with my mother and stepfather, and denied that there was significant racial tension in Fayetteville. But just a few weeks after I committed, he resigned in an explosive press conference where he'd said flat out that he was "judged by a different standard and we all know why." I wasn't trying to tell this guy how much the whole situation had pissed me off, that there were so few programs with black coaches, and that they couldn't seem to just let a black dude live without some drama. I liked Coach Richardson. I implicitly trusted him. He seemed like someone who had my best interests at heart. With other coaches, you couldn't be sure if they were just pretending to care so they could exploit players. But with Coach Richardson, you got the sense, from the way he talked to my parents, my brother, and my coaches, and from the time he spent around my neighborhood, that he really understood where I was coming from.

But it didn't work out. Coach Richardson was battling his own demons in Fayetteville, and when he left amid a dramatic firestorm, I had nowhere to go. It was hard to do, but I called Lute Olson back and told him I would have to reconsider coming to Arizona. "Fine," Coach Olson said, "but you have to come out here. I'm not recruiting you twice."

He didn't have to.

It's a good thing it worked out. Because there was another thing I really wasn't trying to have to tell this man here at this golf club. I had to go to Arizona because once I hit senior year, I only had one goal in my life: to get as far away from Springfield as possible.

Don't get me wrong. Springfield was a fine place to grow up. It wasn't overly dangerous or crazy. There was an average amount of crime and gunplay, always some kids acting wild and certainly some dudes dealing drugs, and all that came with that. But I wasn't really affected by it. Once everyone saw that I had some talent, they kind of protected me. "You can't come with us," they'd say. "You're not about this life." Even my own brother treated me differently, telling me, "You have a chance—you can't be caught up in this bullshit." Even though it made me feel small, it was really their way of looking out for me. I had always been decent at basketball. And I felt like I could hold my own at the playground and in the Boys & Girls Club leagues that were always set up for kids in the summer. I could even play with the project kids who always had a little bit of an extra edge.

But those AAU tournaments were pivotal moments. They were the first validation I had that I wasn't just good enough for Springfield but good enough for the country. The same thing happened the summer I got an invite to a Nike Camp. This time the guys were even better, more elite, but I now had reason to believe that my being there wasn't an accident. When you start to get and seize opportunities like that, the world begins to open up slowly for you. And once it does, it can never close again.

Looking back on it, I can see now how people seemed to never make it out of Springfield. Take Jeff Walker. He was as close to a celebrity as I knew of growing up. I used to love opening up the newspaper, the Springfield *Journal-Register*, and seeing a picture of Jeff flying in the air like a superhero, pulling in a rebound or dunking on some poor kid from a neighboring high school. It was better than seeing Michael Jordan or Penny Hardaway, because Jeff Walker was one of us. Those guys weren't people, they were figures. But Jeff Walker was proof that we could fly too. He was six-five by the time he was a senior and was widely considered one of the best ball players in the country by the time he went off to Iowa. But he was still hanging around with guys who he grew up with. Guys who were not, under any circumstances, good for his career. Maybe he was just too young to see what was at stake. Maybe he had a touch of survivor's guilt, that feeling that because people in the outside world were now taking you seriously you owed something to everyone you came up with. That you maybe didn't deserve the shot you got, so you make penance for your good fortune by constantly giving your time and money to dudes who don't seem to be making it happen like you are. Maybe he just made a mistake. But for whatever reason, he and his homies were trying to run some ATM scam and he ended up dropped from Iowa and facing three years felony probation before he ever played a single minute of basketball for the Hawkeyes. He tried to get himself together at a junior college, but violated his parole by going back to Springfield for Thanksgiving one year. The judge locked him up, and the athletic director dropped him. He bounced around to a few more small programs but ultimately ran out of academic eligibility. You only have so much time to turn a college career into a pro career and Jeff Walker ran out of time. The worst part was that he continued to play at a crazy level. His game didn't fall off one inch. But he couldn't get his head around how it needed to be in order to make this whole thing come together. It seemed to me that Jeff Walker had everything. But it still wasn't enough.

The idea that someone could be as crazy good as Jeff Walker was and still go out like that has haunted me all my life. Because I saw it happening in slow motion, like he was trapped in quicksand and could never get out. But then, Springfield was full of those stories. Steve Dixon. Rich McBride didn't seem to go as far as we would have all expected. Even Frank could have played in the league if he had just figured out a way to take academics seriously. But he didn't. And whenever I went back there, dudes were standing in the same spots, doing the same things they were doing in 1999. They even dressed the same. It freaked me out.

But these towns have an inertia to them. A dangerous lethargy. You meet someone, you get saddled with kids, money is tight, magnificent opportunities are not exactly knocking at your door. You take a job to make ends meet. You realize you'd save so much if you moved back in with your own mother. You mean for it to be temporary, but one thing leads to another. It's insidious. Springfield is a town that if you just let your life naturally occur, you'll be stuck there until the day you die. I liken it to freezing to death. They say it gets really warm and comfortable at the end. You have to have some kind of extra push, some kind of edge, something explosive inside that makes you break out of your downward momentum. Children fight the battles their parents lose. And my mother passed her battle on to me.

Now I looked out at the room I was in. It was not a place you could freeze to death. A golf clubhouse in Arizona surrounded by university boosters. Bright green cacti and mountains the color of faded gold outside while the sun blazed in the seemingly endless sky. You could look out that window and see for a hundred miles. It occurred to me that each of the twenty or so white men assembled in this room probably had more money in their savings accounts right this minute than everyone I knew in Springfield would ever have in their whole lives. And for some reason I was standing among them. Sure, I was an oddity for now. I wasn't dumb—I knew how they saw me: the poor ghetto athlete, probably from a broken home in a crack-infested neighborhood, probably just happy to be in a fancy club with rich people. But I caught myself wondering if someday I'd be not just among these men but equal to them, looking cool and comfortable in crisp golf clothes, an icy drink clinking melodically in my hand and so much money in the bank that I didn't even have to think about it. It seemed impossible. And yet . . .

I was nineteen years old. I didn't know at that point if I was good enough to play in the league. I didn't know that I would be a first-round NBA draft pick and become the face of a franchise and a regular on *SportsCenter*'s "Top Ten" plays. I didn't know that my professional career would span more than a decade. I didn't know that I'd win an Olympic gold medal and be the first player to ever win Finals MVP without even starting. I didn't know that I'd win a championship ring by locking down the greatest player of all time, that I'd play on a team that won seventy-three games in the regular season and then follow it up by playing on what many think might be the greatest basketball team ever assembled. I didn't know that I'd move to the Bay Area, make tens of millions, and be perfectly comfortable playing golf and talking deals with tech billionaires and some of the richest men on the planet.

In fact, in that moment I only knew three things: (1) It was as hot as hell in that clubhouse; (2) this guy I was talking to would not stop asking stupid questions; and (3) this was my only shot. I had to make it work. I had to learn to talk small, for one. But it also meant practice, and study and film sessions, skipping parties, staying away from drugs. Staying up late working and getting up early to do weights and take runs. It meant doing everything it would require to make sure I never had to go back to Springfield. No matter what.

Finally, from across the room, Hassan looked over at me. The two of us held eye contact for a brief moment before we both burst into a full and sudden laughter that we immediately stifled. The athletic director had been clear. We had been warned not to act like fools around these boosters. So we both looked away from each other and pretended to be very serious and engaged. We went back to playing grown-ups.

Stepping onto campus for the first time in Tucson was like entering a completely different world. I had never seen so many white people assembled in one place. It was culture shock of the highest order. It seemed every other kid was driving a BMW 3 or 5 Series. They were everywhere. One girl I was making small talk with casually told me that her father owned like half the gas stations on the West Coast. It was a world unlike anything I had ever seen.

The first place I went on campus was Lute Olson's office. He was in there receiving all the incoming freshmen. His guys. Lute was a real wholesome-looking old white dude with silver hair perfectly arranged on his face and red Santa Claus cheeks. His face looked like it should be on a bag of gingerbread cookies. But underneath all that, there was something ruthless about him. I don't mean that in a bad way necessarily. Just that he was an old-school basketball coach from the John Wooden tradition. He was all business and definitely expected you to be all business too. I would work under his tutelage for two years, and when I was done, I still wouldn't be clear on whether I liked him. One thing, however, was very certain: he taught me the game of basketball like no one else ever had.

But that was to come later. That first meeting was all handshakes and good vibes. The season hadn't started yet and so the staff was still buttering us up like they were recruiting. It was all the platitudes: "Just thrilled to have you aboard. It's going to be a fantastic year! Can't wait to get started!" A couple of goodbyes and it was over. For now. We were given three items of clothing—shorts, a shirt, and a pair of tights—and sent on our way. Just like boot camp, but with Nikes. That afternoon I got a call from a team manager. "Andre, there's a pickup game tomorrow at the practice facility. One p.m."

This, finally, was something I understood. I was excited to get myself situated with the program and show what I could do. For months it had been all this talk about basketball, all this thinking and interviewing about basketball, all this choosing which basketball programs to go to. I was excited to simply go *play* basketball. At 12:40 the next day, we started trickling into the facility in our practice gear. A lot of the guys were players I had seen at various tournaments and AAU events, so there was no real nervousness about that. We started to make small talk and shoot around. And that's when I noticed that I was in a completely different environment.

Arizona prides itself on its team management. The team managers are sometimes seniors on scholarship, sometimes graduates who want to break into coaching, and it's their job to take care of everything a player needs. If you need a ride somewhere, you call the team manager. If you need someone to keep or find stats for you, you call the team manager. But their most important job was rebounding. It sounds like a little thing, but it's the biggest thing there is. If you wanted to get some shots up, it was the team manager's job to make sure that you didn't have to chase the ball all over the floor. And at practice it was even more serious. There was a self-regulated rule in place that no ball could bounce out of bounds more than one time, or else the manager would be in trouble. So even as we were shooting around, there were these guys almost fighting each other for loose balls, running top speed to retrieve them as if they were playing tennis in the US Open. I had never seen anything even remotely close to that. That's when I knew it was all about basketball here.

There were two guys I had never seen before, although I had heard of them. Jason Gardner and Will Bynum. Bynum, especially, was a god in Illinois, as a five-foot-eight dude who could dunk on people. His legend definitely preceded him. Even though it was a pickup game, there were about forty or so people in the stands. Family members who had come for drop-off, others in the athletic program. The seniors Luke Walton and Jason picked the squads, and we were off and running.

I was guarding Luke Walton at first. I thought I was going to be able to contain him with little trouble because, and I'm only being honest here, I took one look at him and thought, "Slow white guy." I was, however, in for a rude awakening. Luke had moves on top of moves. He wasn't going to face you up and cross over that much, but he could get all kinds of shots if you didn't know how to guard him. There were turnaround jumpers, fadeaways, hooks—he had it all. He would wiggle loose on a screen and spot up before I even knew what was happening. Guarding Luke that first game was the strangest experience. You thought he was moving slowly but he was always still one step ahead of you. Even when you knew what was happening, you couldn't stop it. Like when he dribbled hard at you, that meant there was a player doing a backdoor cut. Theoretically you should be able to block the pass, but Luke understood angles so well that he could still slip it by you. He had an answer for your athleticism, but you didn't have an answer for his strength and smarts. He managed to both exhaust me and humble me. And it made me want to learn everything that he had to teach.

The other thing I learned in that game was this: Salim Stoudamire is the greatest three-point shooter in college history. It is a fact you can argue all you want. He did not miss a single shot in that first pickup afternoon. Probably half the time I was losing Luke was because I was distracted trying to understand how it was that Salim still hadn't missed. But it wasn't just that game. It was his whole career. He shot over 50 percent from three in his senior year, and that's volume shooting, that's making 120 threes that season. Only three players in history have made over 100 threes at a 50 percent clip, and Salim Stoudamire is one of those three. And his true shooting percentage—that's field goal, free throw, and three-pointers combined—for that senior season was 68.9 percent. That's insane. By comparison, Steph Curry's true shooting percentage in his best college season was 64 percent. Search the numbers all you want. There has never been, and there may never be, another shooter as purely good as Salim in college.

As the afternoon wore on, everyone got looser. We had made all the jokes, we had shaken all the nerves, and now we were just down to basketball. There was a simplicity to it. It was a game that meant nothing. And that's what made it mean everything. Later I was guarding Hassan Adams. Hassan would be my roommate freshman year, and we would become so inseparable that everyone on campus, including our own coach, would get us confused. But we played the same position, so there was natural competition between us. As soon as we faced each other that afternoon, there was a clear understanding. We were going to push each other as hard as we could. At one point I was guarding him, maybe the third or fourth time we ran it back, and he put a move on me that I still remember. A hesitation, an abrupt little in and out, just enough to get me going the other way, and then he was gone. I was toasted. He drove in to pearl it at the rim, and without thinking I just reacted. I tracked him down from behind and blocked that layup into the tenth row. I just remember somebody saying, "God*damn*!" at the top of their lungs. I didn't need to block it that hard. But I did need to block it that hard. Because that moment set the tone for us, and maybe for that whole squad. We had too much talent and we were going to use all of it.

By the time that game was done, I was a different player. I was in an entirely new world, but I knew I belonged there. Starting from that moment, my old world was completely over.

⸻

The biggest shock of going to Arizona was dealing with Coach Lute Olson. He had a way of being both remote and exacting—a tough combination. It seemed that I could never do anything right for him. And I mean little things. If my foot was at thirty degrees, he'd be yelling at me to make it thirty-five degrees. It was the kind of thing that drove me crazy. I learned basics and fundamentals at Arizona that I would not get anywhere else. And when I finally did get to the league, it was clear, at least to me, that my time in that program and under Coach Olson had prepared my mind for the game in a way that few other guys' programs had. Lute Olson had a gift for taking raw guys, untrained talent, and turning them into professionals. But as an incoming freshman, I couldn't see the big picture. As far as I could tell, he was just a cantankerous old dude who took unusual pleasure in irritating me.

I probably could have handled it better. If you'd asked me then, I would have said I was a player with no ego, but looking back I can see that much of what really got under my skin with Coach Olson was that he didn't let me think I was good. And without knowing it, I had gotten used to thinking I was good. That's really the definition of ego right there. I was nineteen years old and I had one. I remember one practice in particular when I was really just screwing around. I don't know what was going on with me that day, but I was just kind of rolling my eyes whenever he spoke, and Coach was on me bad. It's hard to know which came first. Was I screwing around because he was on my nerves, or was he on my nerves because I was screwing around? Either way, we were not getting along.

He pulled me over to talk to him, and it was the kindergarten balloon situation all over again. I knew that I was in the wrong somehow, but I didn't like being controlled when I was in a certain mood. So I just kind of gave him the "whatever, man" treatment and finished the day without further incident.

After practice, an assistant pulled me aside. "Andre, you know we had scouts here today."

"Yes, OK. Well, who were they here to see? Them two?" I said, gesturing to my teammates.

"What do you mean 'who are they here to see?' Dumbass, they were here to see you!"

What? This was insane to me. Why would NBA scouts be coming to see me?

I knew that I was a good all-around player, but I wasn't even, in my opinion, the best on the team. That honor went to Salim Stoudamire.

Salim was a character and one of my favorite teammates of all time. He was from Portland, Oregon, and was both a Rastafarian and a vegetarian. Salim and I were on the same page as far as education and reading went. We were always exchanging books about black history, race, sociology, African nations. If it had to do with blackness and education, me and Salim were all about it.

We had incredible conversations late into the night about these topics, and it seemed we pushed each other to improve our thinking, our understanding of ourselves, and our pride. It was similar to the way Rich McBride and I had been about basketball, but with Salim it was about politics, revolution, spirituality, and consciousness.

With a guy like that on our team, we were hard to stop. We also had great players like Luke Walton, one of the most fundamentally sound and knowledgeable ball players I've ever known. Hassan Adams and Isaiah Fox, who were my dudes. I loved that team. We hung out together tough, especially because we were on a campus in Arizona that felt pretty far away from home for all of us.

We had a successful campaign in my freshman year, 2002. We went 28-4 in the regular season, won our conference, and made it to the Elite Eight in the NCAA tournament before falling to Kansas. And I felt like we were just getting started. We'd come back next year and go even deeper. Maybe all the way to a championship. It would be just that simple. But as it happened, things that seemed simple in my freshman year got very complicated in my sophomore year.

━━━

It was a process. Going from believing that I was only good enough to play in college to realizing that I actually had professional potential was a process. It took time. As crazy at it may seem now, it was not obvious to me. But throughout my time at Arizona, little moments began to happen, glimmers of hope, of the possibility of something greater for me.

By the time my sophomore year came, I thought I was playing decently. Not great, not transcendently, but decently. My focus was just to do as well as I possibly could. I considered it my job and responsibility to work as hard as I needed to work to satisfy the demands of being competitive in NCAA basketball. And I took that responsibility seriously. In my mind, however, it was not connected to fame and riches and success. I just wanted to be a really good college player, and to know that no one in any program anywhere would outwork, out-prepare, or out-execute me.

But then there were these internet blogs, some of which had mock drafts. "This is what the top of the board looks like if it starts today." That kind of thing. NBA general managers talking off the record, scouts offering opinions.

This was not something I watched closely. So I was surprised when, early in my sophomore season, a teammate was looking at his laptop in the locker room one day after practice and called out to me.

"Yo, Dre, you on this draft."

"What draft?"

He showed me. There I was. Some website had me going in the first round. It was odd. Kind of an out-of-body experience. My first thought was, Are they talking about another Andre Iguodala?

I shrugged it off. The internet, sports guys, media—they never know what they're talking about. Just a lot of bullshit to get clicks.

A few days later I was coming out of the arena after a game. It was one of those cool Arizona evenings. The sun was just beginning to disappear. And there was a guy waiting for me. Kind of unassuming, mild-mannered. Black dude. A little square. Didn't really make much of an impression except for the fact that he stopped me as soon as he saw me.

"Hey, Andre. How you doing?"

"Um. Fine . . ."

"Hey, I'm just letting you know who I am . . ." He told me his name and that he was a sports agent out of Chicago.

I froze. I didn't quite know what the rules were, but I was worried that even standing next to this dude meant I was violating some type of NCAA something or other. It felt like a sting operation.

He saw my face and chuckled. "Why you looking at me like that, dawg? Don't worry. I'm not giving you anything. Not breaking any rules. I'm just saying hello. I think you're a good player."

"Thanks, but I don't think I'm supposed to talk to agents. I'm not trying to get in trouble."

He was understanding. "No, of course. Don't worry. We're going to do everything the right way. I'm interested in you and I think you're a good player."

"Interested in me for what?"

We exchanged phone numbers and started to stay in touch. And I began to warm up to him. After games we would text. He'd tell me what to work on, what I was excelling at from his point of view.

During one of these conversations, he said something like, "The way you played tonight, that's why teams like you."

"I'm confused."

"What are you confused about?"

"I mean . . . Coach has been telling me that I have to get much better. That I have to work on my game."

"That's because he doesn't *want* you to leave, man. You don't see that?"

I didn't. I simply hadn't thought of it that way. Here I was, just trying to please my coach and match, to the best of my ability, the standards he had set for me. And it never occurred to me that he might have an agenda that was completely self-serving. Even though it had happened before, on my JV squad, I still was surprised to have it happening at the college level. I shouldn't have been. But I was. Apparently, I had a lot to learn. After that, everything changed. A problem began that would plague me for nine or ten years. Sleep deprivation. Insomnia.

It is difficult to describe to someone who hasn't experienced the intensity of insomnia. It is like you are being tortured by time, by something that moves slowly and doesn't care for you at all. You put your head on the pillow every night with the hope that if you somehow pretend that it's all going to be OK, you can make it so. Maybe you even get so far as to close your eyes, let the silence fall over you, and drift into a kind of temporary sleep. But then an unwanted thought intrudes. A memory of a bad pass or a missed jumper. You start to think about what Coach would say. You start to remember tough moments from practice and wonder if they'll hamper your career. You start thinking about what it will mean to your career. To your life. It feels like everything is hinging on doing everything right, and you feel like you'll never be able to do everything right. And those thoughts, though fleeting, give you just enough adrenaline to shoot your eyes open and accelerate your heart.

And now you are awake. Staring the whole night in the eye. The clock ticking. You watch game film. Play video games and PS2. Try to get quiet enough inside to salvage what's left of the night. But just as your fear is finally running out of fuel, the morning comes. And you know it's too late now. You have to get it together, you have to get dressed. You have to face another day.

This began for me once the specter of going pro became a real thing. And it continued intermittently for nearly a decade. Maybe it began then because this was the precise moment that basketball went from being a game to being a business.

It seemed that time sped up after that. Now I had to make a

decision about what to do. Should I declare? How do I handle the draft? What about grades? Should I finish college? What if I go to a bad team? What if the scouts are wrong and no one wants me? What if I play badly and lose my chance to go pro? It is one thing to play in order to meet your own expectations, or the expectations of your teammates or coach. But once it feels like every shot can make or break your career, and you're just nineteen years old? That's a different kind of pressure. Between that and Lute Olson, my confidence was getting messed up.

And I was starting to feel the difficulty of dealing with the press. In my sophomore year we made it to the Pac-10 tournament in Los Angeles. Tournaments are tricky for a player because everything is different. You're not just coming from your dorm room or a hotel to play. It's a little more chaotic. You are staying in a hotel, but you're back and forth to the arena all different days, and your schedule keeps changing. If this team wins, go here at 11:00; but if this team wins, go there at 10:00. Meanwhile other games are going on all around you, press is there, fans and hangers-on are wandering around everywhere. The whole scene is just kind of crazy. So we were getting ready for a game, there were two more games ahead of us, and I realized that I had somehow forgotten my socks. With so much going on, I had just spaced. I left the locker room and hopped on the phone to my girlfriend to ask if she could go back to the hotel and swing by to give the socks to our equipment manager.

I made the call in this little corridor between the locker room and the court.

She came by with the socks and everything seemed fine. We ended up winning but I did not have my best game. I wasn't too bent out of shape about it; it happens sometimes. I would get 'em next round. At least we advanced.

The very next day on the front page of the sports section there's a photo of me talking on the phone with a caption implying that I was distracted and making personal phone calls seconds before taking to the court. Now, this was a good ninety minutes before our tip-off. And I was on the phone for all of forty-five seconds. But somehow the impression was made that I was on the phone only thinking about myself at the team's most critical moment. What did people think I was doing? Making shoe deals? Agreeing to appear in a rap video? I was just trying to get some socks.

The next day Coach Olson was pissed and yelling at me. And that's when it clicked. That photographer, those reporters, they were doing their jobs. They were just trying to make their money and I just happened to be standing in the right place to be a target. They're literally looking for any story at all. And I unwittingly had given them one. And now Coach could use that against me. "See, he's not ready!" Then the word gets out to teams. "Iguodala? Yeah, he's a good player but is he mature enough? You heard he was on the phone distracted right before he played in the tournament, right?"

It was too much, and I started asking myself why. Why was I facing this pressure? What was the point? I was learning how to play, but I was also getting yelled at by my coach, low-key hounded by agents. I was starting to feel trapped, like other people owned me. Even though I was not big man on campus, and I wasn't on the cover of every magazine, my sophomore year saw me spreading out a little bit. Gaining a little bit of a name. Students I didn't know were beginning to come up to me. "Hey, Andre. Please stay a little longer." At one point the athletic director, with whom I had never exchanged a word in my life, walked right up to me like we were best friends. "Hey, Andre. I hear you're thinking about leaving," he said. I didn't understand how we suddenly got on a first-name basis.

After a while it starts to wear on you. It's subtle but insulting. Kids on campus were wearing my number and the school was getting forty to fifty dollars for each jersey sold, but I still was playing in exchange for "tuition, room, and board."

I began to think about what it all meant. One of my favorite things growing up was to look at old Fab Five tapes. People routinely underestimate how much impact those five young men had on the game of basketball, and how we, as young players, viewed ourselves within the system at large.

We felt like Juwan, Jalen, Chris, Jimmy, and Ray represented us. They represented the possibility of black people having a voice in college basketball: a billion-dollar market where our bodies were the labor but our personhoods were unwelcome. They were Blackness against the Machine. We loved their style, their swagger, and their phenomenal success. We loved how much certain people hated them, said they "didn't play the right way" and were "disrespecting the game" by wearing black socks or baggy shorts, or having the nerve to believe in themselves. White fans at home might have bought that argument. But I can assure you that every broke and struggling black ball player from Tallahassee to New Haven, from Virginia Beach to Compton, saw that for what it really was. A lot of people simply don't like it when black kids feel powerful. It threatens them. Once a black person exhibits that they have no need for white approval, then suddenly all manner of hate and insults and threats come in. It's always masked by terms like "respect" and "tradition." But the way we saw it was that it was about power. The power to achieve your maximum greatness on your own terms. The power that comes with not giving a fuck about white establishments.

The other piece of media I was obsessed with that year was the film *Blue Chips*. Sure it's a little campy, but to be quite honest, *Blue Chips* was dope to me when I was nineteen years old. If you haven't seen it, it's a basketball movie starring Shaq, Penny Hardaway, and Nick Nolte. There's also plenty of cameos by basketball legends like Larry Bird, Bobby Knight, Jerry Tarkanian, and Rick Pitino. And lots of drama. High-speed real-game sequences, moral dilemmas—what more could a nineteen-year-old obsessed with the game possibly ask for? The story revolves around a fictional college team in Los Angeles that is struggling. The coach, played by Nolte, is on the hot seat after his first losing season. Encouraged by a shady booster, and despite his own moral doubts, he pays three top high school prospects to commit to the following season. He ends up with the best freshman class in the country, but the guilt is too much for him. After their season-opening victory over Indiana (with actual footage of Bobby Knight on the sideline), Coach admits that he cheated and quits his job. The way the movie is told, it's all about Nick Nolte's character. But the way I saw it, it's about the recruits. And, besides Spike Lee's *He Got Game*, it was the only film I had seen up until that point that truly showed how dirty the collegiate athletic business could be, and also the only one where anyone makes a real argument for why you should pay kids that play in college. A booster makes a point to the coach early in the film that colleges owe this money to kids. Sure, the moral of the story is that you should follow the rules. But I've noticed over the years that the people screaming the loudest about following the rules are always the people who benefit from them. I took another moral from the movie. I saw myself in these kids and I gained a greater understanding about the game.

That movie got me thinking about how much the programs were making. Not just in ticket sales, but in TV rights, jerseys, concessions. And that's not even mentioning how much sports helps with enrollment, tuition, and branding. We were literally wearing the school's logo on us every time we walked in front of a camera. We're one step from being branded with the school name. I was also being asked to help Arizona with recruiting. I was responsible for showing guys around campus and convincing them that this was the right place to be. So in addition to playing for the school and working in the marketing department, I was on the admissions staff?

That was a large part of the reason I began to think about leaving early. I began to look at it as if I was working for any company, say Google. I've been an employee, I've done my job. But then it becomes clear that there are career-advancement opportunities available to me if I strike out on my own. Of course I want to test the water, want to make sure I'm making the right decision. But once I get a sense that there's a better deal out there for me, then I'm going to start looking into it. Wouldn't you?

So I began to break it down. What was my compensation from the University of Arizona? OK. I'm getting an education, of sorts. Technically. And for me, I was getting much more of an education than a lot of guys on my squad. I was All-Conference Academic my entire time there. I left with a 3.0. I was actually *going* to class, doing my homework.

The education really can help if you are an athlete who knows that you are not going pro. That would be a great thing *if* guys on teams were actually getting an education. But when you look at big-name, multimillion-dollar programs, you've got to be honest. It's not about education. It's about sports. And that's it. It's about getting guys in and getting guys out so the teams can compete next year. And if you're a player on one of those teams, your whole life is basketball. You're up early in the morning at the gym, running, lifting. You're practicing, you're traveling. The toll on your body is intense. You're getting fatigued, injured. Every waking moment is consumed with either practicing, playing, or thinking basketball.

And yet you're supposed to carry a full course load and get an education. I'm not saying it's impossible to do. I did it. But I was in a position to do it because I was already a real student coming in. I had already taken high school academics seriously, been in honors classes. I did that because that's the kind of person I was. But it wasn't because the school cared. They would have recruited me regardless, so they can't take credit for the fact that I happened to be a student. They cared that I remained eligible, that I was not in violation. But they did not care if I got an actual education. That's simply not what college sports is about.

The guys who are being recruited are being recruited for their basketball skills only. Some of us are coming from situations where no one has cared for a moment about academics in our entire lives. I've played with guys who can barely read. I've seen guys literally have all their homework completed by "tutors." They don't care because the goal is not to educate young men, but to sell tickets, merchandise, and the logo. And those kids' bodies are what is traded in exchange.

There's a scene in *Blue Chips* where a bunch of coaches have descended on a Chicago Catholic school to recruit Butch McCrae, played by Penny Hardaway. They are all in the office waiting to make their pitch to the principal, played by Lou Gossett Jr. When he emerges from his office to see all these men assembled to compete for the services of McCrae, the principal pretends to be holding a slave auction. "How much for McCrae?" he asks sarcastically. "Young boy, good stock, strong, hard worker. Where can we start the bidding?"

That is how it has always felt to me on some level. Sports is people telling you to use your body to make them money. In professional sports you are receiving a paycheck in exchange. In college you are not. But why is that? In college they are still generating income.

Collegiate administrators can say that they're providing you with an education in exchange, but if they are recruiting kids who are not students, looking the other way while those students take bullshit classes and have their homework completed by tutors, and then letting them walk before they graduate, and they're letting all that slide *specifically so those kids can stay and play*, then how can the exchange of goods honestly be said to involve an education?

The tuition is worth $25,000 to $65,000 per year, depending on the school, but the most recent NCAA men's basketball tournament generated over $1 billion in revenue this past year. Coach Mike Krzyzewski at Duke currently makes $8.9 million per year. Coach Brian Jones at North Dakota State, who is one of the lowest-paid Division I coaches in the country, made a reported $109,273 in 2017. Even that salary is worth way more than the average price of an education. And that's not including bonuses. So the athletic director is making seven figures. The coach is making seven figures. The assistants are making six figures. TV networks are making billions. And yet the players who are grinding their bodies into nothing, sacrificing kneecaps and ligaments on a daily basis, who are the only people anyone tunes in to watch, are earning the equivalent of $40,000 per year? And that's not even in cash but it's in a "service"? That's like being offered the most physically dangerous job on a staff where everyone else is making six or seven figures, and you're supposed to risk your health and be the face of the company for a compensation package of $40,000 in gift certificates.

NCAA basketball claims to care about its student athletes but doesn't make it possible for these athletes to support their families, who are oftentimes struggling. A basketball player has to play for free for at least a year, a football player for three years, before they are eligible to earn an income. But sports like tennis, baseball, golf, and even hockey allow kids to go pro whenever they want. Is it a coincidence that these are overwhelmingly white sports while basketball and football are not?

When you take all that into account, Jalen Rose wearing black socks is not the person who is disrespecting the game.

So, when I added all this up, the choice was pretty clear. NCAA basketball is a racket. And the players are the only ones losing.

That was what began to become clear for me from the moment that agent started talking to me outside the arena that night. People who say that agents talking to kids interferes with the purity of the game are being disingenuous. There was no purity to the game to begin with. It's just that oftentimes the players are the last to know.

I wanted to make sure that, out of respect, I told Coach Olson before I went public. I sat down at his house for a dinner he invited me to. It was awkward. We'd never had anything other than a relationship totally about the execution of basketball. I was sitting at his home—which was beautifully appointed, looking like something out of a movie about rich people. I felt certain I would break a $60,000 vase or something. We fumbled our way through small talk punctuated by uncomfortable silences as best we could. His wife, apparently, had had enough.

"Andre," she blurted out, "are you coming back?"

"Oh, well . . . I don't know if Coach wants me back."

Coach Olson jumped in. "Well, of course I want you to come back, Andre."

It was a stunning moment. Never, all year, had this man expressed anything close to that. All year it had been "Grow up. Play better." No positive reinforcement at all. Now all of a sudden I'm part of the family?

But I was realizing that there was a reason he was doing this very poorly executed wooing right here and now. He needed me. If I did go pro, he'd need me to be on his side. He'd need me to stay connected to Arizona basketball to help with recruiting.

But I needed him too. GMs were going to be asking him about me, and one word from him could sink my career if I rubbed him the wrong way. One word could cost me millions.

We sat at that table, no longer player and coach, no longer kid and mentor. Now we were two men, one black and nineteen years old, one white and seventy years old, engaged in a transaction on equal footing.

I laid it out. I told him that I was going to be moving on. That I appreciated everything he'd done for me, but that it was a dream of mine and I had to go for it.

He was quiet for a moment. "I respect your decision" was pretty much all he said.

M y time at Arizona went by so quickly that it almost felt like it never happened. I had come to campus hoping to have an entire experience. Instead I found myself confused, unsure, and pushed into things before I was ready. My basketball got better. But in the end, college was not the place for me. If you are to play like an adult, you should be paid like one. Whether I was ready or not, I had seen the signs. It was time to move on.

04

Welcome to the NBA

The first agent I spoke with was the guy who had stopped me outside the gymnasium and told me that Coach was holding back on how good I was. In the time that had passed, he and I had kept an informal relationship going. It was exactly what I needed at the time; a perspective outside of the program and outside of my own head. He was doing what agents do: making himself available seemingly out of charity, but in reality grooming me as a client. His goal was to make it so that I felt like I couldn't possibly imagine navigating my career without him. And in a lot of ways, it worked. I was at least 99 percent sure that I would sign with him. But although I didn't know much, I knew better than to sign anything without due diligence. My experiences with college recruiting had taught me nothing if not that. I let him know that I was going to, just as a formality, talk to a handful of other agents.

"Yeah, no, that's great," he said. "I get it."

"Yes, thanks. I just want to make sure I do it the right way. Best-case scenario, I sign with you. But I want to go out and learn a little more about everything."

"Of course. Totally understand."

"Cool."

"Just . . . you gotta know all these other guys are bums, man. They can't do for you what I can do for you."

"Bro, relax. I'm going with you. Chill."

"Yeah, no. We're good."

"Cool."

"Just don't trust those LA guys man. They may look flashy, but they have too many clients. You'll be bottom of the barrel there. With me—"

"Man, I said I got you."

"'K. Cool."

I did my due diligence and met with a handful of other agents including another group out of Chicago. They flew me out to Chicago to meet with them, and they were making the solid pitch. I had been flown out, dined, and courted. They wanted me to see the facilities where their athletes had access and show me a little bit about the town. We were riding in the back of a limo, making small talk, when my phone started to buzz with texts.

"Man, how's it going?"

It was the other agent, the one I had told to relax.

"Pretty good, bro," I replied, hoping that would end it.

"Cool. You should come by the office since you're in town."

"Nah, man. Look, I really wanna do this the right way, after all the stuff I've been through the past few months. I'm not trying to be disrespectful or go behind anyone's back."

"Cool, cool. I can respect that."

Then a minute later I received another text. "I'm going to drop by your hotel tonight."

This guy wouldn't let it go. Then he begins to tell me about how the people I was meeting with, right there in the car, were trash and how I should never trust them.

It was stressing me out. And despite myself, I mumbled out loud, "Man, these guys are always hating."

The agents knew exactly who was texting me. Then they started trashing him. The whole thing just bummed me out. I've never been one who responded well to pushy people. I'm not someone you can fast-talk into a corner. Usually the pushier you are, the more you trash other people and pump yourself up, the less I trust you. It's just not a style that works for me. Making the decision to leave school had been stressful, though I knew it was the right thing to do. But the world outside seemed even more treacherous. I really began to feel like I didn't know who I could trust.

The final agent I met with was Rob Pelinka out of Los Angeles, and what we did during our meeting was play Ping-Pong. That was it. That was what did it. Ping-Pong. No talk of business, no talk of basketball or branding or other agencies. He didn't tell me how he was going to make money off me, what he had planned. He just asked me about my life and told me about his. It was the first time in the whole process of looking for an agent that I could just relax. I didn't feel like I needed to protect myself or be on guard about anything. He treated me like a human being and not like a cash cow.

There is so much dehumanization in big-money sports. A lot of people don't want to hear it because of what we get paid, but money doesn't change that fact. It really makes it worse. Money really makes people look at you like an object. You're putting your body on the line, and no human body was meant to run up and down the court for eighty-two games. You get injured, you take a cortisone shot, you're back out there. I've been told that I'm a "hard-nosed player." This is supposed to be a good thing. Once, I broke my hand in a game, stood up, taped it, and went back out to play. Coaches are like, "Atta-way! You got heart!" But honestly? That's some dumb shit, playing with a broken hand. In this game, people are all over you, trying to get in your head and manage your thoughts. And that process is intensified when you're a new prospect.

So, playing Ping-Pong with Rob, just having someone treat me like a person rather than an object, really worked for me. That night I slept better than I had in months. The next time I saw Rob, I told him I was going with him, and that was that.

"Great," he said. "Now here's our plan."

Rob had found out that there were a handful of teams that didn't like me. One didn't like me from the cell phone incident. Another's scout had seen me giving Coach Olson bad looks in that freshman practice. Rob's plan was to fix my rep with these teams. And he wanted to do it by going through Coach Olson.

We set up a meeting with Coach, and that's the first time I got to see Rob work. He had a great instinct for what Coach needed to hear and also for how to increase my brand and perception in the eyes of NBA front offices.

"Coach, oh man, we just want to thank you for everything you did for Andre. Without you, we wouldn't be here. Whatever you need, let us know. Andre's Arizona for life. We're going to come back every year. Whatever you need for camps. You need us for recruits, we'll call the recruits. There's nothing like an Arizona guy being a pro for recruits."

It worked. Every GM, every scout, every assistant who called Coach about me heard nothing but good news. "Andre's a hardworking player. We've had no issues. Good teammate. Here's what he's working on." That meeting with Rob made all the difference. Because without it, the story very well may have been, "He's a good player but he can be a little difficult at times. Here are a couple of examples . . ." The difference between millions of dollars can be just that subtle.

I began to work out in Chicago in preparation for team meetings. Rob set me up with a number of players, both aspiring and current NBA guys to train with. But the biggest influence in that whole group was a midcareer guard named Corey Maggette. Corey was a six-foot-six small forward from just outside Chicago playing for the Clippers at the time. The thing most casual fans remember about him was that he could get to the free throw line more than anyone else. He was consistently a leader in the category. But his teammates called him Maximus because it was widely known that he approached his practice like a gladiator. He worked out with incredible discipline, and he ate like a monk. As a kid just coming out of college, I was completely ignorant to the level of physical and mental discipline it took to remain in shape for the longevity of an NBA career. As far as I knew at the time, all you had to do was lift and run around. But Corey was incredibly specific about diet, about supplements. He tracked his heart rate, calculated formulas. He was not only a scientist with it, but he also physically pushed himself harder than anyone I'd ever seen. It was one set after another, more sprints, more weights, more shots up. I had never seen anything like it, and it changed the way I understood my body and my profession.

After that, it was back to Arizona for three weeks to finish classes and wrap things up at school. Returning to campus was weird. It suddenly hit me how fast everything was happening. When I first stepped on campus for freshman year, I had truly thought I'd have more time to just be a kid, to be a basketball player in college. To go to parties and play pranks on campus. I remember once I showed up to a costume party in a diaper and people thought it was hilarious. But that second year, and the sudden attention from scouts and agents, the cooling relationship with Coach Olson, getting dinged in the press, and maybe most importantly coming to realize how incredibly lopsided the game was for so-called amateur athletes, had forced my hand. I was ready to take on independence, and I was ready to look forward. But there were moments on that visit back to campus when I felt envious of how everyone else got to hold on to their youth a little longer. Kids were biking around, sitting in the quad in flip-flops and shorts with no greater decision to make than what they were going to get from the dining hall in an hour. It seemed that everything had happened to me so suddenly. But what had been done had been done. There was no room for those moments of doubt. So I made no room for them.

Next, it was to Chicago to work out with Tim Grover. He was widely known as Michael Jordan's trainer and he was the guy you had to see if you were serious about the draft. It would be an understatement to say he had a reputation. He was known as the toughest trainer in America. I got a little apartment in downtown Chicago. My agent, Rob, loaned me some money to live on that I paid back without interest over the next six years. And from there, my only job was to eat, sleep, and live basketball.

I showed up for my first workout with Tim at 6:00 a.m. on a Monday morning. I was confident that I could do what needed doing and, even though 6:00 a.m. was a little on the early side, I arrived ready. Grover looked exactly how you would expect a trainer to look: like a fit corporate executive dressed to take his kids out on the weekend. Athletic clothes but not a hair out of place. His T-shirt was tucked into his shorts. Anytime a guy's giving you drills and his T-shirt is tucked into his athletic shorts, he's going to give you hell—you can count on it. I took a deep breath and dove in.

The first drill seemed simple enough. Run around a half circle, pull up, shoot. That was it. And to this day I don't know what it was—the hour of day, the pace he had me at, or the way it was designed—but literally halfway through the first drill, I honestly felt as though I could not continue. It was like I was five years old and trying to keep up with a grown man. My legs were dead, my arms were Jell-O. I have never before or since doubted my decision to go pro more than I did in that moment, in a cold Chicago gym at 6:15 a.m. I knew that no matter how much I wanted to quit that I could not. It was one of those defining moments in my life. Everything in my body told me that I could not do this. But everything in my will told me that I must do this. There was no choice. I would have to find it somewhere inside me.

I tried to hide how much I was struggling, but Tim could tell right away.

"Harder than it looks, huh?"

"Nah, I'm good," I could barely get out.

He said nothing.

I pushed and pushed until the drill was done. It seemed like it had been forever, but it had been less than five minutes. I put my hands on my knees and realized that sweat was already dripping down my face and back.

"Good," he said. "Now let's get started."

don't know how I made it through that first day with Tim, but somewhere along the way, everything else disappeared. I mean, all other options evaporated. It was just me, my body, and my spirit in this gymnasium. And once I fully accepted the totality of that moment, I became capable. I didn't have the words for it then, but it was one of the first times I truly learned about settling my mind in order to help my body. Making it through that first day felt like an unimaginable victory. And when the second day came, I walked into that gym without a shred of doubt.

I lived in Chicago alone for all those weeks and my entire life was basketball. I was within walking distance of Tim Grover's gym, so my world became very small. And I liked it. After feeling all the pressures of dealing with creepy agents, weird coaches, and dishonest press, there was a peacefulness to being so narrowly focused. Wake up. Walk. Train. Eat. Train. Walk. Eat. Sleep. I wish it could always be so simple.

My first team workout was with the Chicago Bulls. They were looking at two players: me and a Sudanese kid out of Duke named Luol Deng. Deng was rangy and quick. Skinny but tough. The knock on a lot of players out of Africa at the time was that they were a little soft, a little fragile for the American game, but I didn't see that at all with Deng.

I thought my first workout went well. I was feeling energized, sharp. Satisfied. But back then they would make you take a psychological profile. I don't know how medically accurate it was, but they seemed to take it seriously. It was multiple choice, and then a few short-answer character questions.

After the workout I sat down in an office with the GM and a few others.

"You tested pretty well, Andre, but we were wondering . . . what . . . uh . . . what makes you tick? What makes you go? What makes you mad?"

"Um, well. I just like to play hard. I don't really get . . . um, mad? I guess."

"So, you don't get *angry* on the court?"

"No. I just . . . I just play hard. I push myself and play to win. I mean, I guess if I'm losing, then I'm mad."

"Andre, have you ever smoked weed?"

"No. Not at all." Which was the truth.

"You can tell us if you smoke weed, Andre. Everyone's tried it at least once. We've all tried it. We know how it is."

"Yeah, no. I really don't smoke weed. I have no idea at all about weed. No idea. If you put something in front of me I wouldn't even begin to know what to do with it. I barely even know how to turn on a lighter."

"Andre, you can be honest with us. We understand that you might be nervous, but you don't have to be. A lot of guys smoke. I mean, if you have a problem, we'd like to help with that, but you don't have to hide it."

"I don't smoke weed, man."

They switched tactics.

"Listen. We think you're a good player. We think you're with it. But we wonder if . . . well, if you have enough *grit*."

"I mean . . . you just saw me work out. You just saw me bust my ass out there. You've seen all my tapes. So, I don't really know what else I can tell you."

"OK, OK. Thanks, Andre."

That's how it went. It was a very strange interaction and a little discouraging. I felt like they were looking for something very specific, and I simply wasn't giving it to them.

After I worked out for a few more teams, the Bulls called me back for a second look. I went alone. This time, there were no other players. It felt this time like they were trying to kill me. I was doing full-court stuff nonstop. Jumps, crawls, sprints. Suicides. They were trying to break me to see if I would quit. But I kept it together. Another good workout, another meeting.

This time they got straight to the point.

"We like you. We think you're a good player. But we don't know if you have enough . . . grit. We need to see, basically, if you have some . . . killer in you."

"What . . . do you mean?"

"Well, you've got great grades in school. You did your homework, and we looked at your background in high school. You were an awesome student. If you were my son, I would think I was the perfect dad. I would be an unbelievably happy father. I did my job. But this is the NBA, and it's like you kill or be killed. We want to know if you're a killer out there."

How exactly are you supposed to prove to a roomful of white men that you have some "killer" in you? Grab a knife and start shanking people in the office?

"Yeah, I don't know. I let my play do the talking."

In the end they went with Luol Deng and a point guard out of Mount Vernon, New York, named Ben Gordon, both of whom were good players and both of whom had very nice careers.

But another team would find exactly what they were looking for in me. And the next eight years of my life would be spent in Philadelphia.

⸻

I t all started well enough. When I met with the 76ers team before the draft, it was as easy as it could be. It helped that they were drafting relatively late, at the number nine spot, so they weren't even sure if they would get me. So they spoke with me candidly. "If you're still there," they said, "we're taking you." It was straightforward. My meeting with them didn't feel like an interrogation, possibly because they weren't sure they'd even have a shot at me. It was very basic: here's our scheme, here's what we'd want you to do, and hopefully we'll see you.

This was good. It meant that I would not arrive in Philadelphia with a lot of pressure. When you go high in the draft, you get a lot of team-savior expectations placed on you right out of the gate. You're going to a bad team. You're the big star. You're supposed to come out on the first night and single-handedly change the fortunes of an entire geographical region. This is hard for players, and it's not great for teams either. Picking first or second in the lottery can make a front office go haywire. Now they have to analyze every single thing about a player. Psychology, background, etc. When a front office is picking high, they really have to get it right, otherwise fans turn on them, owners turn on them, and they could be out of a job. High draft picks are a lot of pressure. But the 76ers were picking ninth, so they could afford to just draft for the best talent. If it didn't work out, and they had to trade the player or something, no one was going to storm the office with pitchforks.

But there were warning signs. One of my closest friends was from Philly. And once I got drafted, he told me, "Yo, Philly's kind of a different type of place. You know, the media's kind of crazy a little bit. They can be a little rough." I heard him, but I can't say it really landed for me. I had gone to school in Arizona, where the press is more or less on your side. In high school I hardly saw any critical press coverage at all. I could hear his words, but it would be a while before I knew what he *really* meant.

You would think that draft night is something you'd never forget as long as you live, but the reality is that it's such a circus that you don't really fully understand what's happening. It's a blur in my memory. There is such an unusual feeling of fear and excitement. I was trying to keep it together, because the reality is that none of it made sense to me. Here I was at Madison Square Garden, twenty years old, just a handful of weeks off a college campus, months away from thinking that I was going to play college ball for four years. It was a lot. I could feel my hands tingling, my body stiff. I tried to eat but the food tasted like cardboard.

I was clearly going to get drafted, so why the fear? It's just butterflies brought on by the grandeur of the moment, the production of it. There are a million assistants and network people and NBA officials running around, tech crews and caterers. There are families and friends, loved ones and little brothers and sisters, and everything seems to be happening all at once. You're waiting in a room with all these other guys, and it can be uncomfortable for some people.

Eventually we figured out that the camera comes toward your table, and that's how you know you're getting picked. There was a moment when I saw them walking toward me, and I thought this was going to be it. I sat up straight, adjusted my tie, and prepared myself to meet my future. But I was mistaken. They were coming to talk to the guy whose table was next to mine: Rafael Araujo out of Brigham Young.

But a few minutes later they came for me. I was led away from the waiting area and to the side of the stage. From the wings I could see how many people were in the audience. It was overwhelming. And then I heard those words, the ones you dream of for your entire life. "With the ninth pick in the NBA draft, the Philadelphia 76ers select . . . Andre Iguodala, University of Arizona."

I walked onto the stage and was blinded by a rash of cameras. I shook David Stern's hand and received my 76ers hat. My life changed instantly. I really mean it. I was whisked off right away to do a press blitz that lasted nearly two hours. I didn't get to see my family or my friends. Suddenly there's this entire world set up, all these reporters and fans and officials. I went from not being a part of something to instantly being at the dead center of something very huge, an entire organization with a staff and a history. I went from being my own to belonging to an entire city. The next day, they sent me to Philadelphia to do press there, and the first interview I did, I was chewing gum during it. It had never even occurred to me not to do that until Lester Conner, one of the assistant coaches, pulled me aside and told me not to. I realized that I had a lot to learn about the press.

Despite this hoopla, I didn't expect to mean a whole lot to the fans in Philadelphia. My vision for myself was never to be the face of the franchise; it was just to be a nice piece for a team that wanted to contend. And I expected that because the Sixers had a player named Allen Iverson. It's true that the Sixers and Allen, specifically, weren't coming off a great year, but he was still the man in that town. He had the franchise on his back, and as I would learn later, he was expected to carry the success or failure of that team all on his shoulders. I wasn't even expected to start. They already had Glenn Robinson installed as the small forward, and he was coming off a good season.

Pressure was also low for me because of a general East Coast bias. Most national sports media are based on the East Coast, so it's easier for them to follow East Coast players. Out west, we might be tipping off a college game at 7:00 p.m., while it's already 10:00 on the East Coast. These sportswriters are half asleep by then—they're not staying up till 1:00 a.m. to watch you play. You hear a lot about the ACC, the Big East and Big 10 Conferences, so out west you're kind of under the radar. Nobody in New York was checking for a player in Tucson, Arizona. Basketball people knew who I was, but for the average fan, Andre Iguodala was not a household name. This was a good thing. No mythology around me, no expectations.

With this in mind, I arrived at training camp in North Carolina. We were working out at Cameron Indoor Stadium on the Duke University campus. Being back in a college gym helped me feel even more at home, and I knew what to do. Play hard, play defense, and try to relax. I knew the fundamentals of the game, and I was going to put them to good use.

In scrimmages I was facing Robinson, the starting forward we called Big Dog. He had been a standout at Purdue in the 1990s. I remember watching him play when I was growing up, and he was a real beast. He was a big, solidly built man who talked in a slow, patient way. Almost like a southern grandfather. And he was incredibly strong, could finish at the rim, and had a real nice sense of the game. I felt humbled to be in his presence, and he was incredibly nice to me. A lot of players want to haze rookies, and when that rookie is at your position, sometimes the hazing can become cruel. But Big Dog never had that vibe. Like me, he was an even-tempered Midwest guy, and he treated me well throughout that whole camp.

I was trying to learn everything I could from facing him. And he was good. Very good. Crafty. Some of his moves reminded me of what I had seen in Luke Walton at Arizona. He would do little things that frustrated me, rubbing off on screens, knowing how to stick his hip out just enough to disrupt you when you were trying to go over top. It was occurring to me that veterans played this game completely differently than rookies did. They seemed to get more done with less movement. I wanted to learn that.

Glenn could score, but as camp progressed, I saw that I could score too at this level. My attitude against him defensively was to let the coaching staff and my teammates know that I came here to make a difference. I think for the coaching staff they saw that I was not going to be an offensive liability. And this was important because it meant teams couldn't cheat off of me by doubling Allen Iverson. This was a good strength to add to my defensive skills, which I could demonstrate right away. Team defense is about attention, but individual defense is about attention plus effort. And while I was still learning the ins and outs of his particular game, I knew effort very well.

I had first learned how to play defense at a young age playing against my brother. I told you what he was like on the court. Ruthless. Playing against him for all those years forced me to defend aggressively and quickly. But I was also motivated by a desire to set myself apart from every other kid on the floor. Whether it was at school, camp, the Boys & Girls Club, whatever, I always wanted to win. I wanted to be the best at everything. If we were running sprints, I wanted to be first. Who had the most points? Who had the most rebounds? In my mind, it should always be me. And I wanted to be the best defender too. It's just competing.

That's why Scottie Pippen was one of my favorite players growing up. I loved Michael Jordan, of course, but Scottie was the guy I

watched most closely. He could do everything, and he was all business and effort. Very little flash and magic. But he made the whole
thing work. He had a swagger that came from confidence, from
knowing you're just going to outwork everybody else on that floor. In
a lot of ways I modeled my game after his and Penny Hardaway's.
Especially in those high school years when I was tall but bringing the
ball down the court to initiate the offense. Guys would shout, "There
goes Pippen!" I can't say I minded the comparison. I loved Michael
Jordan just as much as everyone else, but Scottie Pippen was the guy
I related to.

At the end of training camp, Jim O'Brien, the head coach, called
me over to him. "Andre, we want you to start," he said. I couldn't
believe it. He had barely looked up from his clipboard, but the words
landed on me like a ton of bricks. I played it cool. "OK. Let's go play."

This is really when I learned what the NBA was all about. The
next thing I knew, Glenn just wasn't on the team anymore. I didn't
come in trying to take a guy's job. I was just trying to hoop. He had
been kind to me, never showed any animosity, never any sense of ego.
It really felt weird to come in here at twenty years old and put a
grown man and a veteran out of work. It's not something I celebrated.
It was a difficult situation for him: "We don't need you anymore." He
was essentially told, "You can go find another team, or you can wait
until February and we'll buy you out."

The whole situation grew awkward after that. We were back in
Philadelphia practicing at the College of Medicine, where our training facility was. If you could call it that. It was one of the lesser facilities in the league. We'd come into practice, head downstairs to the
locker room, and Big Dog would be lifting weights there. But he
was not on the team anymore. I didn't know if we were supposed to
say, "What's up?" to him or what. It was incredibly weird. I didn't

understand why he couldn't even come off the bench, but he didn't. They just told him to beat it. We saw him around the facility for like a week, and then he was gone. That's when I learned that this business was ruthless.

———

My first regular-season NBA game was against Boston at the Boston Garden. November 3, 2004. A lot of people might say it was overwhelming to be in such a hallowed place, to hear your name over the PA system, but I wasn't really thinking about it. I just remember reminding myself that I came to play, and play is what I was going to do. This was going to be the culmination of everything I had worked for. I was prepared. I had spent the summer working out with Tim Grover, so not only was I in shape, but I had been banging around with NBA guys for months before I stepped on that floor.

That night I got to face Paul Pierce. I was already a big Paul Pierce fan, and playing against him only made me more so. I got to see up close what a genuine master he was. He had such a wide array of moves that it was almost impossible to predict what he was going to do. It was clear that his game was the result of consistent work and practice, and I really gained a tremendous amount of respect for him.

Paul didn't say a whole lot to me that first night, and I certainly wasn't trying to get him going, so I kept it quiet for the most part. But he was one of the most devastating trash-talkers of all time. If you and he were battling, like really going blow for blow, he didn't say much. And we had some truly great battles over our careers. But if you were weak and had the nerve to bark at him, he would make you live to regret it. He had this funny thing he did with lesser players who couldn't keep their mouths shut. Because there are some guys who have to talk to get jacked up to play. Like I said, it's competition, and whatever gets you going gets you going. And sometimes a young fella would strut off the bench and start, for whatever reason, talking trash to Paul Pierce. And Paul would say nothing. No response, no retort. At least not at first. Instead he'd wait until we were all gathered around the free throw line. And then when the game was quiet enough for you to hear someone slurping beer in the third row, he'd say at the top of his lungs, "Listen, if you don't make more than ten million dollars, shut the fuck up. You can't talk, bro." There really was no coming back from that. Even your own teammates would be laughing and shaking their heads at you.

My first NBA game was a success for me. We won by 2 points, and for my part, I played well. I knocked down my first couple of shots, even hit a three early on. I don't think anyone on that floor expected me to shoot threes, but I got in the flow of the game early and just let it rip. I just wanted to win. I just wanted to prove I belonged. Somehow, I knew deep down that this wasn't going to be one of those things where I'm here for a couple of days and then gone, telling someone ten years later at a barbecue how I once played a few games in the NBA. This was going to be a long journey. Despite all the fanfare, despite the Boston Garden, despite Paul Pierce, despite finally hearing my name called in an NBA game, despite everything, that first night to me was just business.

Every night in that first season, I got a chance to play against someone new. That is the most tremendous part of your first season in the league. The first time I got to play against Shaq, I was awestruck. Or Yao Ming—it was amazing. And for me specifically, it was Rip Hamilton. I was a tremendous fan of his from his days at UConn. In a lot of ways, I was more of a college basketball fan growing up than an NBA fan, and I rooted for Rip when he won the championship with the Huskies. So when we played Detroit for the first time, I was kind of starstruck.

"Yo, that's Rip Hamilton," I said to Allen Iverson. "His game is nice."

"Yeah, he's much better than people think," Allen replied. "An All-Star for sure." Then he paused and looked at me. "But he breathes the same air you breathe."

This was something Allen said a lot if you ever got too starstruck. He would kind of joke with you about it: "This man breathes the same air you breathe." That's the way he saw things. You were to give your opponent respect, but not too much respect. "You're a killer just like they're a killer," he would say. "So go out there and kill them." And that's the way I saw him handle himself. When he went out on the court, his whole goal was to show everybody that there's nobody better, or even *close* to being better, than him. And that was every single night.

He had a reputation. He had a lot of reputations. But there was no one ever like him. He played with a recklessness that I've never seen. He was driven in a way that very few guys are. You've got people like Kobe who are assassins. You've got people like Michael Jordan and LeBron who are crazy athletic and very determined. But Allen Iverson was pure motor, pure will. There was hunger to his game that you can have only if you come from where he came from. It wasn't competitiveness or ego, although there was some of that. At the core, it was just pure, honest hunger and an absolute refusal to be intimidated.

He also had a reputation as a ball hog, but what I actually saw playing with him was that he had to trust you. It was a sense, sometimes misplaced, of ownership he felt over the game. In his mind it wasn't up to the coach or the scheme or the clipboard. When he was on the floor, he was in charge. He really had to believe you were good or else you weren't getting the ball. It put a lot of pressure on the guys around him, because unless you were playing well, he figured that his chances of making the shot were better than yours, so he was keeping it. For him it was a pretty simple calculation.

When I started playing with him, I would, on my off nights, read about him. I wanted to know a little bit about who he was and where he came from. Mostly I looked at a book called *Only the Strong Survive*, by Larry Platt. And really, Iverson's Hall of Fame speech eventually said it all. Rats and roaches in the house. Sewage pipes busted, walking through shit and piss in his own house. This was a guy who came from some serious struggles, some life-or-death things, so he wasn't someone you could bully by getting in his face on a basketball court. He simply did not give a fuck.

But the thing that probably most people don't understand about Allen Iverson is that he is wildly intelligent, incredibly quick-witted and multitalented. He was a cartoonist. He could draw you, a portrait of you, just out of memory. And he'd put a big bump on your head or draw you with a fat lip. He was always making everyone laugh. And he could rap. Like really rap. I know a lot of guys think they can flow, but Allen could really freestyle and pull verses out of thin air. He'd take a rap song and turn it into a country song just off the top of his head, and the whole bus would be singing along. He could make up choruses on the spot. He was never short with a joke, no one could outwit him, and he could throw a football like seventy yards. I've seen him do it. He had a stunning kind of charisma and an intense sense of self that people who played with him couldn't help loving. He was just gifted in life. And that was on top of the insane things I witnessed him do on a court. It was like God gave him extra talent.

I was always cool with our coach, Jim O'Brien. He was straight to the point and did things his own way. He was all about his own rules and philosophies of the game, and it was pretty much his way or no way. Overall this was a very good quality, especially for me as a rookie needing to learn the rules of the game at this level. Sometimes coaches will want to give their players freedom, which can be a good thing. But what sometimes ends up happening instead is that you have no idea if you're making the right or wrong decisions, and you lack clarity on if what you're doing is working and why. This can be difficult for a young player. But Jim, by contrast, valued clarity. He knew how you were supposed to run every play, and if you messed up, you knew exactly how and why you messed up.

He was the first coach I ever met who was entirely obsessed with stats, well ahead of the rest of the league. He would know the statistical efficiency of every possible combination of players, and he spent hours poring over numbers and advanced metrics. It was impressive, and sometimes very useful. But there were times in which his consistency could get us into trouble. This is why guys gave him the nickname Half-a-Head. Because sometimes it seemed he could make decisions with only one side of his brain.

We were playing at Toronto sometime in the last third of the season. Coach had cooked up a defensive scheme for us based on what he saw working statistically. And obviously you can't defend the whole floor at once, so he made it clear to us that in this particular game, he was willing to give up a three-pointer from the left or right sideline. Not necessarily the corner, but a little farther out, around the twenty-four-foot mark, where they are much harder to make. He knew that this was statistically the most difficult place to shoot from and that this was this was going to give us the best chance of winning. Things were more or less working according to plan for the first seven minutes or so, until Donyell Marshall came off the bench for the Raptors. Marshall had been something of a journeyman at that point, on his tenth year in the league and having played for more teams than I could count. He was never known as real shooter—his lifetime average from three was in the mid-30s, which O'Brien undoubtedly knew. We didn't feel we had to overcommit defending him on the perimeter.

We were wrong. Donyell and the coaching staff had clearly figured out where our sweet spot was, and a few minutes after checking in, he spotted up from that sideline and drained one. Thirty seconds later, he did it again. I just remember someone on our team—I don't know who, might have been Michael Bradley—yelling, "Oh SHIT" as soon as he realized Marshall was open again. A few seconds later I hear "Oh SHIT" one more time, and Marshall is draining his third three from that very same spot. At this point it was clear that what O'Brien was doing wasn't working. Donyell Marshall was forcing us to adjust. But Coach was having none of it. All that stat study meant that once he had a plan, he was sticking to it. There was simply not enough time to research another one. "It's going to work," he kept telling us. He figured that Donyell was just on a streak and would have to, sooner or later, regress to the mean.

I guess if Donyell was going to regress to the mean, he wasn't going to do it that night. He made shot after shot after shot after shot, all from the exact same spot on the floor. When it was all said and done, he had made an NBA record 12 threes in a game, which stood untouched for eleven years, until it was broken by my now teammate Steph Curry. Guys on our team were mad that night. We hated getting burned like that, but overall I can see where Coach was coming from. It *was* a statistical anomaly, and for the most part, Coach's understanding of defense, informed by stats, was way ahead of where the league was at. He was an excellent first teacher for me.

I got myself through those early years by trying to learn from my veterans. And we had some great ones on that team. There were guys like Aaron McKie and Kevin Ollie. They didn't have the most talent, but they managed to be on their tenth, eleventh year in the league. That's someone worth learning from, as far as I was concerned. We had Corliss Williamson. Corliss had just come from Detroit and showed me my first-ever championship ring. I could not believe how big it was! I still get chills thinking about it.

I learned from some guys who were on the straight and narrow, and I learned from some guys who showed me what *not* to do. I remember one guy I played with, late one night after a game when we were approached by a fan. I could write a whole chapter about the crazy things fans do and say, but suffice it to say that while I'm grateful for them, they were not always easy to deal with. We'd get a lot of groupies, women approaching us, but it was more men than anything. So this particular night we were out, it was about 1:00 a.m., and we were approached by a fan who wanted a picture. And this player was like, "Why are you asking me for a picture? There's all these women out here. Why you don't ask one of them for a picture?" At the time it struck me as cruel and unnecessary. I mean, this guy was just trying to support our team. I made a decision that I would never be that way with fans. And to this day, I really haven't been. But I have to say, as the years have passed, and I've been a part of some real media circuses . . . I can't say I *agree* with that player's behavior, but I understand it more now.

That first season seemed to blow by. There was so much to absorb, so much to adjust to. We snuck into the playoffs as the seventh seed in the East and managed to win only one game against Detroit before being eliminated. It was not a great season for the team, but I felt I played well and stayed focused. I was back in the gym before the finals were over.

Despite this, the real joy for me was always the guys I played with. Aaron McKie was one of my favorite teammates ever. When I got there, I started to try to figure out who's who and what made these guys tick. And Aaron struck me immediately because he dressed well and carried himself with a certain stylish confidence. He used to wear these Prada loafers, not hard-bottomed but kind of a hybrid, dressy but sporty. And I always thought those really summed him up. On my first day on the team, he invited me to his house and I watched him play poker. It's a great way to see how someone maneuvers, how someone splits the difference between where he was from and where he was going. Aaron was from Philadelphia, and while he stayed connected to his roots, he was also able to keep it professional. That street stuff didn't really go on in his presence, and he made sure of that.

Even though we played the same position, he was generous with advice. In the Eastern Conference alone, I had to guard LeBron, Paul Pierce, Vince Carter, Joe Johnson, Michael Redd—the list goes on. Aaron put me onto the game as far as the proper attitude to take into facing these guys. "Look," he'd say, "they're going to score. There's a reason they score twenty-five points a game. You're going to get bad calls on you. You're a rookie—the refs aren't going to let you reach in. Your job is just to make them work as hard as possible for those twenty-five points. If they score twenty-five but are exhausted at the end of the game, then you've done well."

Aaron taught me how to understand the bigger picture of guarding great players. You have to make them work. Some nights they'll get the best of you no matter what you do. Other nights you'll be able to slow them down somewhat. But the way Aaron explained it, the goal was never to shut them down every single game, because that would be impossible. What you were really trying to do was to build a reputation for yourself. You were trying to make it so that after a while, everyone coming to face you knew that you were going to give them trouble.

This is one of the areas where the 76ers organization excelled in my first year. We had a great front office with great scouts. Early in the season, Frank and T.J. Zanin (they were brothers) were scouts for our team, and they gave me a DVD of the top small forwards in the league: Paul Pierce, Richard Jefferson, Tracy McGrady, Vince Carter, and Carmelo Anthony. It was just forty-five minutes of all their moves. I watched it religiously, pretty much every day. I was told to work on those moves, and I probably emulated Paul Pierce the most. Back then a lot of the game was about working on isolations: you'd find your sweet spot on the block and go into your set. If you watch old Carmelo tapes, you'll see he was a master at this. So I'd watch for hours and then do their exact moves in my workouts. I wanted to get the choreography in my body so that offensively I could perform it naturally, and defensively I could guard against it instinctively.

After a while, the game begins to make sense. Every team in the East was more or less working off the same framework, and so really you'd have to learn just the variations. And you wanted to pick up on it quickly because if you didn't, they wouldn't hesitate to find someone who would. I watched a lot of film. Sometimes I'd watch nearly the whole game all over again before the next date, to figure out what I did right, what I could do better. I got used to approaching things that way, with a certain amount of thought and care, and I first learned that in Philly.

Another guy I loved playing with was Samuel Dalembert. Sammy D was funny. We were teammates for many years, and he was a unique dude. He was a good basketball player, and as one of the best shot blockers in the league, he was able to earn himself a pretty nice payday. But he had one of those minds that was hard to focus. Kind of a genius type. He was Haitian, grew up in Canada, and was fluent in a couple of languages. I always got the sense that he ended up in basketball because of his height. Like if he was six-two he probably would have been a math professor somewhere. That's not to say he wasn't good. He had a nice jumper, was a very good shot blocker, could run like a deer. But he had a host of other interests. Unlike a lot of guys, basketball wasn't his life.

One of the craziest things about Sammy D is that he could make computers—from scratch. He was the only NBA player I ever knew who could do that. And we got pretty close over time, so at some point I needed a laptop and I was looking online trying to find one. I asked Sammy for his expert opinion. He was offended. "Man, don't do that! They'll charge you a bunch of money for software and a lot of shit you don't need. I can build you your own personal computer for half that."

That sounded good to me, so I told him I was with it. A few weeks later, Sammy unveils my machine. A beautiful computer that had everything I needed on it. It was decent. A year goes by, I'm on a flight, I open up the computer, and the thing just crashes. Like expires. Corrupt software, all kinds of nonsensical messages.

I go back to Sam like, "Sam, what is this about the computer, man, what happened?"

He's like, "Oh, the software expired."

"What do mean expired?"

"Yeah, it was a free trial for twelve months."

"What? Man, I could have just bought a new computer for all this trouble!"

This guy got me a computer with bootleg software and acted like it was all legit.

But it was hard to be mad at Sam. He was very easygoing, always smiling, always laughing. People used to criticize him for not taking anything seriously, not having a killer instinct, but you have to look at where he came from. His beginnings were very humble, and he made it all the way to the NBA. If I were in his shoes I'd be smiling and joking too.

Then there was Willie Green. Willie ended up as one of my coaches at Golden State, but back then he was what you'd call a pro's pro. He learned the game from Kevin Ollie and I learned a lot of it from him. Willie Green was very clear about the things you need to do to stay in the NBA. At six-three, he was in a tough spot as an undersized shooting guard. To compensate, he played hard every day, every practice, every game. If he had to break your leg to get minutes, he would. But he did it respectfully, as funny as it sounds. He would tell you, "I'm going at you today." And you knew what that meant. Willie would elbow you in the mouth and just look at you like, "Sorry, man. I gotta eat." It didn't matter that he was your teammate, Willie would straight up take your lunch money. Nonetheless, I always respected him. He made the most of his talent, because he could have easily been the kind of player who'd be in the league for two or three years tops. But he got over a decade out of himself and he built a reputation as a player who did not fool around. If you messed up, he'd tell you straight to your face.

Another no-nonsense guy was Marc Jackson. I'm not talking about the point guard, former Warriors coach, and announcer Mark Jackson. This was Big Marc, the center. This was a guy out of North Philadelphia, and he'd never let you forget it. He put "NP" on his ankle tape, so he could tape his socks up high and make sure he was always representing where he hailed from. He was another one of those guys who gave me a lot of good instructions and advice.

I had my brother and cousin with me a lot that first year. They were something of a small entourage, for lack of a better word. And I mostly stayed on top of my business, but one practice I was fooling around with them and we showed up late. Really, in my whole career I've only been late to one practice, and that's probably because of what happened next. When we walked in that day, Marc Jackson went right at my guys and cussed them out. "Y'all in the house? What y'all doing? Neither one of you got jobs! So if Dre don't eat, y'all don't eat. You are his alarm clock. Don't you ever let him ever be late to practice ever again!"

I was shocked. But the funny thing is, I find myself saying that exact thing to young guys now. Marc influenced me a lot, not so much about basketball but about how to operate your life off the court with the minimum amount of trouble. He would make sure all of us young guys knew how to keep situations well attended to, whether it was business, women, or friends. It was really street smarts that he made sure all of us had. He had something of a sixth sense for how a basketball life should operate. He was like a manager of entourages. He made it clear that it didn't make sense for me to rush home from practice to get the cable hooked up or have to spend time that I could be in the gym on little errands. Every NBA player has some dudes they grew up with hanging around them, and Marc was really good at seeing that for what it was. A job. Everyone wants to wear a suit and do business deals all the time, but someone has to do the grind work of keeping the operation going so that everyone can eat. Marc helped me understand that.

I also had the good fortune to play with Chris Webber for a couple of those years, and this was a real thrill to me. Chris was really the reason I started watching basketball in the first place. When he played with the Fab Five at Michigan, I was glued to the TV set. So when it all came full circle and we became teammates, it was a surreal moment. He came halfway through the year and took my number (4), I wasn't fazed. I gladly took the number 9 out of respect for him, and I still wear it to this day. He was coming off an injury then, so he was in that phase of his career where he was just trying to hold on. And the conference did him no favors. He was facing Kevin Garnett, Rasheed Wallace, guys like that, on a nightly basis. I watched him struggle and the toll this game took on his body. He took a beating and it clearly affected his mood. When he had a good game, he was in a good mood, but after a bad game, he took it hard. Chris was a thinking man and a very emotionally intelligent one, and very conscious of the black experience in America. He has a great collection of African American art and artifacts and we had many conversations on the black experience and black wealth in America. He was at the tail end of his career, so he was a little more quiet and reserved. I truly admired our conversations away from the game. C-Webb should really be a Hall of Famer, and he knew that, and I think those games where he struggled impacted him deeply.

Another guy I really learned a lot from was Elton Brand. In my later years, under Coach Eddie Jordan, we signed Elton Brand to a big deal. He came off an Achilles injury but was looking to make a go of it in Philly. I can be honest and say that we didn't hit it off right away. I'm not sure that he was enjoying the situation with the 76ers. He was not a great fit for the system. They were trying to make him a "stretch four" of the type you're likely to see nowadays. A big man who can move on the perimeter, guard smaller guys, and knock down jumpers. But that just wasn't his game. He was an old-school block player. Don't let him back you up under the basket and get to his left shoulder. He'd toast you every time with that. But Eddie's system didn't really allow for a lot of that. So after a while, Elton took matters into his own hands. In the middle of a game he'd just be like, "Fuck that—I'm going on the block," and he'd get his points that way. Which I understood, but it kind of screwed up our whole set. We'd just be standing around watching him work. I can't say I enjoyed that at first, but I get that he was in a tough position.

But after about a year and a half, he became one of my favorite teammates. We sat down and had dinner. He was very open and forthright about the mistakes he'd made earlier in his career, especially where money was concerned, and he wanted to make sure I did better than he did. He was another guy, like C-Webb, who knew a great deal about black history and always looked to educate himself and the people around him. I will always treasure those dinners I had with Elton. I grew to respect him a lot. He was very much on point.

In a lot of ways, it was Elton Brand who changed my life. He was deep into black history, a very educated man who was always reading, always studying deeper concepts. He was the first person to really make me understand the difference between money and wealth. Back then, there was Will Smith, Oprah, Michael Jordan, and Bob Johnson, who had just bought the Charlotte franchise, and Chris saw a pattern. He recognized early that we were coming upon a time when black people could begin to seize the means of production, not to just make money for ourselves, but to own stakes in the biggest transactions. Now you see that happening. You see Jay-Z and Diddy moving to own the media companies that make money off black talent. Everyone is thinking bigger these days. Michael Jordan showed us that it could be done for oneself, but Chris Webber was the one who showed me it could be done for the culture. He fundamentally changed the way I thought about my career and my money.

I had a lot of great players beside me in Philadelphia and I grew close to those guys. Many of them are still in my life today. But for some situations, great guys aren't enough. The reality is that my time with the 76ers had a will of its own. And no matter how hard I tried to avoid it, things were going to head in a certain direction for me. There was simply no way to resist it. I couldn't control it. Instead it controlled me.

NO CAVITY CLUB

ANDRÉ Iguodala 7/12/93

JAMES R. SANTARELLI, D.D.S.

Clean teeth . . . until free will kicked in.

Left: Eighth grade. First pair of Air Jordans.

Above: Before I grew into my ears.

Look of surprise as I was caught—probably up to something sneaky.

Above: With mom dukes before I headed to a high school dance.

Right: Junior year of high school, all skinny arms and legs.

High school varsity team, when I was still a "hidden gem."

2001, College Signing Day, when I originally chose Arkansas.

With my big bro after the draft.

Above: Freshman year at University of Arizona.

Photo courtesy of University of Arizona Athletics

Right: With my brother from another, Rich McBride.

Rookie photoshoot. An amazing feeling.

Familiar scene in my younger days, playing in the 2010 FIBA World Basketball Championships in Turkey. Although Father Time has been good to me . . .

Getty / Garrett Ellwood

The 2010 FIBA World Championships are one of my most memorable basketball experiences. A couple of the guys became future teammates.

London 2012 Olympics. One of the greatest teams ever assembled.

Sneaky kid (like father . . .) sneaks in Hamptons Five photo.

First "Shampionship"
(in the words of my man
Leandro Barbosa).

Getty / Jesse D. Garrabrant

Left: Headed to the White House with my wife to celebrate our first championship with President Barack Obama.

Right: Fashion has been an interest of mine since I was a kid. This was at the 2015 New York Men's Fashion Week kickoff party, hosted by Amazon Fashion and the CFDA.

Onstage with Sarah Lane at TechCrunch Disrupt SF in September 2015.

At the Annual Players Technology Summit that I launched in 2017.

Photo courtesy of Gene X Hwang/Orange Photography

Rich Kleiman, myself, Kevin Durant, and my business partner Rudy Cline-Thomas
at the Players Technology Summit 2018.

Photo courtesy of Gene X Hwang/Orange Photography

Celebrating our 2017 Championship.

05

The Most Hated Athlete in Town

Jim O'Brien got bounced after that early exit, and next season we came back to a new coach, Maurice Cheeks. We played with Mo Cheeks for the next three and a half years, but we only made the playoffs with him once. Nevertheless, Philadelphia had a lot of love for him because he was part of the 76ers' glory years. As a point guard, he played on a team that went to the finals four times and won it all 1983. And he played with Dr. J, Charles Barkley, Moses Malone, all the greats. He and I had a good relationship, but the fact is we struggled under Mo, and I watched the environment in the locker room become more and more difficult the more we lost.

So less than two months into the 2008–9 season, Mo Cheeks was fired. He was in his fourth year as our coach, but we were off to a 9-14 start, and I suppose the front office had seen enough. The assistant GM, Tony DiLeo, was promoted to interim, and we were able to clinch a playoff berth that year. Still, we lost to Orlando in the first round, and the team made a decision to bring in Eddie Jordan to coach. Eddie was a good guy and, to his credit, arrived with a good attitude and ready to work. But from the start, he was in a very tough position. His first order of business was to try to install a Princeton offense, which can, under the right circumstances, be truly great. It's a four-out, one-in with a lot of backdoor cuts, dribble handoffs, and spacing shooting. It's not set. You have to make the reads based on what the defense is giving you. Sometimes they call it the "motion offense." If a player is denying the ball, you dribble at the guy. It's an automatic backdoor read. If a guy is overplaying one way, you go this way. If he's underplaying, then you pop back. It has a triangle feel to it—always moving, always cutting, always adjusting.

The problem with it is that you need Princeton players, and we didn't have them. It takes time and patience to build and install an offense like that. Philadelphia was remarkably short on both. Steve Kerr says it takes two years to install an offense, and if you look at Golden State, that's exactly what happened. We won seventy-three games the second year of Kerr's offense. It took us that long to get it fully embodied. These schemes are mental and physical and kinetic. You can't just learn it off of a whiteboard; you have to learn it in your body, you have to play game after game after game in order to see all the variations, all the wrinkles, all the counterattacks. But Philadelphia didn't have the patience for it. The fans were booing us after like the twentieth game. Three months in, the front office was ready to scrap the whole project. Eddie did the best he could, but, man, I didn't envy his position.

Philly fans can be tough. I remember when Elton Brand got hurt one year. He tore, essentially, his entire shoulder out of the socket. It was a gruesome injury. And when he was working his way back, naturally his production wasn't what it had been. There was this one fan, believe it or not, one guy who would blurt out how much money Elton was making per game. You'd hear him in the middle of the game yelling, "Elton Brand is making four hundred sixty-five thousand dollars tonight, and he only has two points and two rebounds." The thing is, we never sold out unless it was a big game, so you could just hear this guy as closely as if you were in the same room with him. "Andre Iguodala is shooting thirty percent from three. Why did he just shoot a three?"

Willie Green got it the worst. This guy would heckle Willie nonstop. "Oh, here's Willie Green with the ball again. Why is Willie handling the ball? I don't know why you got Willie Green on your team!" Finally, one night I had had enough. I was running by him and I just said, "Yo, man, shut up. Don't say another word about him, man. Please don't say another word." I was back down the court before he could respond, but you have to push an athlete pretty far before he's ready to bark back at a fan. I've actually heard about players having to send a family member over to confront a fan about disrespect.

Once, we were cruising along late in a game up by 15 points. Midway through the fourth quarter, the other team made a little run and cut our lead to 9 points. Our fans started booing! We had to call a time-out. There were boos the whole time-out. I had to look at the scoreboard to make sure I was seeing things correctly. We were up by 9 points and about to win at home and our own fans were booing us?!

Those were the situations that made you grow up quickly. I came to understand players like Allen Iverson a lot more as I grew up in the game. "All of this is on me," he once confided in me. "If we lose, I'm the person who's going to get blamed." At the time I'm not sure I understood, but after a few years of dealing with those fans, I started to get it.

You had to, in a sense, protect yourself from the press too. Allen Iverson always told me to never read the paper, which of course sounded silly to me. I had a newspaper with me all the time when I was a rookie. I hardly even read the sports pages. I was reading current events, maybe knocking out a Sudoku puzzle or two. Until one day Allen saw me doing that and told me, "Don't read the paper, bro. It'll mess up your game." Over time I could see that he was right. Certain players on our team would get branded by the press—this guy can't shoot, this guy can't post up—and those parts of their game would slowly deteriorate. They may have struggled with it a little to begin with, but the branding was the nail in the coffin. They didn't want to even try it in games, because they were worried about what the press would be afterward. It made you a little bit guarded. You have to stay on your p's and q's when you deal with the press because these guys' job is to look for a story, and they don't really care how it impacts your actual life.

Allen understood that better than any of us. He would warn all the players who were starting to find themselves gaining the attention of fans and press. During the Olympics, he told Carmelo, LeBron, and Dwyane Wade, "This shit is sweet now, but y'all boys better be ready for when they turn on you, because it's definitely going to happen." He would tell me the same thing. I'll never forget it. He was like the old guy in a horror movie who warns you at the beginning that there's something evil in the abandoned house. And of course, he was right. Every single one of those guys got attacked by their own fans at some point in their careers. Even me.

One day I was sitting at home with the TV on in the background. ESPN was playing a segment where they were ranking the most hated athletes in every city. When they got to Philadelphia, guess who it was? Somehow Andre Iguodala had become the most hated athlete in his own city. It was upsetting, and surreal. You think about how much you've tried to work and be as professional and successful as you could be. You think about all the times you played hurt, all the times you gave literally everything you physically and emotionally had to get a victory and put on a good show for the fans. You think about those times you drove to the basket, got mauled by some seven-footer, crashed elbows-first to the hardwood, made the bucket, got the foul, and stood up boosted by the fans cheering for you. And here you are, being told you're the most hated athlete in your town.

I'm sure some of it had to do with my contract. After the first four years, I signed a contract extension: six years for $80 million. And it really changed everything. Those first contract years were great. I was a young guy, and there was very little pressure. I felt spry and free, bouncing around, really just having fun and balling. Allen had all the pressure. My contract was a rookie contract, close to the league minimum. For the team, this is a winning arrangement. The rookie scale is so low that if a team gets a guy who's really good, it's like paying the minimum for a superstar.

In the 2015–16 season, Steph Curry made a mockery of the NBA single-season record by making 402 threes. (The last non–Steph Curry to hold the record was Ray Allen with 269. That's how good Steph was in 2015–16.) That same year, he was a unanimous MVP, went to the NBA Finals, and won it as the best player on his team. Safe to say he balled out that year. But there were fifty-three guys in the NBA making more than him. Including me, to be honest. I had him beat by like $400,000. Paul Millsap was making more than Steph was that year, Khris Middleton was making more. Reggie Jackson was making more. A contract isn't always tied to how you are currently playing. While Steph was literally rewriting NBA record books, there were guys coming off the bench making more than him. You get paid for how you played on your last contract, not your current one. So when Steph signed his deal in 2017, and it was worth about $201 million over five years, he was being paid for everything he did from 2012 on.

For most athletes, the big contract is when all the struggles with the fans and the press really start. Fans have a weird logic to it. Let's say you're on your rookie deal and you're averaging a solid 15 points, 10 assists, and 10 rebounds. These are good, productive numbers. Once you are up for a new deal, you're going to get paid. Let's say your next deal is worth three times as much. By some people's logic, you're now supposed to be playing three times as well. You're supposed to be averaging 45, 30, and 30. What's not taken into account in this expectation is that the rookie deal was a bargain for the team. You were getting paid way under market value and earning half as much as vets who are producing less. That's what it means to be a rookie. You can't suddenly pull numbers out of nowhere. Steph was making $11 million per year when he shot 402 threes. Now he's making a little over $40 million a year. Would you now expect him to shoot 1,608 three-pointers this season? It makes no sense. But sometimes people do assign this same logic to lesser scenarios. And I know there are some guys who sign a deal and then disappear, but that's not what I was doing. I remained consistent, a regularly improving player who worked nonstop to get better. My best points-per-game, assists-per-game, and rebounds-per-game seasons were all after I signed my deal. But somehow it wasn't enough. I'm not going to turn into Michael Jordan meets Kobe Bryant meets Wilt Chamberlain overnight just because I signed a contract. I'm just finally getting paid what the market says my production is worth.

As my time in Philly wore on, the media began to bother me more and more. It was hard to know who the real culprit was: the fans or the press. In a sense, to an athlete they become two sides of the same hypercritical coin. Beat writers and talking heads drum up stories, and in Philadelphia, negative stories simply moved more units than positive ones. Fans then parrot these talking points, and pretty soon you find yourself being criticized from all directions. Even for the most stalwart of players this becomes too much. Especially when combined with the tremendous toll your body takes crashing around for eighty-two games per year.

The experience of being an athlete became more complicated. It was a blessing. By waking up every day, playing basketball, doing what I had loved doing since I was a kid, doing it at the highest level, and getting paid handsomely to do it, I was quite literally living a dream. There are so few people in the world, so few moments when a person can stop and say that the life they have right then is exactly the one they dreamed of having. But that made it much harder to understand why it was that it was so difficult, why I felt so bad sometimes. I was doing exactly what I wanted to do. Why were there moments when I started to feel unhappy.

Soon I found myself growing mistrustful of the media. I hated press availability, that period before and after games where you had to be present for interviews. I started to gain a little bit of an edge, to answer questions in as few words as possible. You can see press fatigue in an athlete's eyes in a postgame interview. Even the way it's physically set up can feel dehumanizing. You've just played an entire forty-eight minutes of basketball. It is late and you are tired. Your body aches, your knees and joints burn, and you've just suffered a loss. Your frustration is at an all-time high, and that's the precise moment in which seventeen reporters pin you against a wall in the locker room, with no escape, surround you with cameras and microphones, and start picking apart your best efforts. So you, understandably, feel frustrated. You start to give one-word answers and speak entirely in platitudes. After a while you just want to play ball.

Each media market has its idiosyncrasies in terms of what kinds of stories and characters they fall in love with. Philly, as a perpetual underdog city, a cold concrete and brick city, a city always in the shadow of New York, has a certain soft spot for those gritty guys, those longshot guys who go against the odds. Think Rocky training for a championship fight by punching raw meat in a walk-in freezer. This, in large part, is why Allen was such a star, at least initially. Here was this skinny six-foot-one pit bull of a player who wouldn't back down from anything at any time. They really liked that. He had a personality fans could easily attach a compelling story to. But simply put, that was not my deal. I was not going to do and say dramatic things publicly. I was maybe a little quieter, a little more focused on production. But I also wasn't going to sing and dance, shake hands with and smile for the press. I respect the way AI did things. He was true to himself. And I tried to be true to myself. We were different personalities. And soon I was being labeled "distant" and "aloof."

In that way, Allen's time as the reigning athlete in Philadelphia cast a long shadow on my own experience. He had a complex, contentious relationship with the press. It was very much a love-hate thing with him. When they loved him, he was the second coming of Christ. But when he went rogue, they killed him. The press and fans were primed for a dramatic relationship from the moment he left and I took over as the face of the franchise. It felt as though they were looking for a drama with me that wasn't there. And eventually, the fact that it wasn't there became the drama. In 2012, I woke up one morning to find that the *Philadelphia Inquirer* had written an entire article comparing me to Philadelphia Eagles quarterback Donovan McNabb. Like him, I was called "aloof"—I wasn't as engaging with the crowd.

I tried to not let this stuff affect me, but that's nearly impossible. Some guys become contentious and want to quit on their teams and fans. Some guys want to do stuff to ingratiate themselves to the fans, because they have a hard time with anyone thinking badly of them. In a situation like this, everyone goes deeper into what they know. What I knew was work. And work became the container, the vehicle, for all the energy, frustration, resentment, and ambition these events triggered in me. I found myself trying to prove myself every single day, playing extra hard, putting in a tremendous amount of effort. I had been criticized for not being the leading scorer even though I was supposed to be team leader, so I started to occasionally break a play, exert myself to get extra points, or to rack up extra rebounds so I didn't have to hear the next day about how I wasn't earning my paycheck. But I would still be going extra hard on defense because this is what I prided myself on. Sometimes my teammates were like, "Dog, you alright? You're overexerting yourself. Let us help you." And I'm saying, "Let *me* help *you*!"

There was a darkness to my situation, to my thinking during these years. What began as a court situation ultimately became a life situation. I became obsessed with working out to nearly unhealthy levels. I threw myself into lifting weights. Normally you lift two days a week; I was doing it five. All I cared about was getting shots up, spending every day in the gym. Going as hard as I could at all times. I wasn't talking about it in the press, but I felt compelled to push myself as hard as I possibly could. It was just what I thought I had to do to prove my worth. I was killing myself mentally. I wasn't taking breaks. I was always tense, always pushing. My whole life became about proving wrong the people who doubted me. I didn't want to talk to anyone. I didn't want to be a part of anything that didn't involve a gym. I shut myself down. My life became very small, and I had a hard time finding any kind of joy in anything.

In those dark hours when I couldn't sleep, I would lie awake in the glow of a television or a computer screen and turn plays over and over in my head, thinking about what would have happened if I had made this pass or taken this shot. I became as familiar with the night as I was with the day. I knew what time certain sounds happened. A dog barking, the newspaper landing on a neighbor's steps. The silence that surrounded it was deafening. All I wanted was to enjoy the game of basketball again. Now I felt like I had grown old enough to feel the weight of an entire world on my shoulders, but still without the power to manage it.

During the day I tried to make a good show of it. When I look at interviews from that time, I can see that I was smiling *more*, trying to sound *more* upbeat. I didn't want anyone to know what I was going through. I thought that if I could manage it well, if I could will and work my way out of it, then everything would be alright.

But you could tell. I was growing my hair out and avoiding almost all social engagements. All I cared about was being at the gym. It was wake up, work out, get shot after shot after shot up, go to practice, lift again, take more shots, then go home to sit alone, or invite one of my friends over to just shoot the shit. I sincerely thought that I was doing what I was supposed to be doing. This is what I had learned. Work hard, keep your head down, don't complain. But I was in a situation where that advice was no longer good enough.

I was averaging nearly forty minutes per game for those final seasons in Philadelphia. I've always been someone who said I don't believe in minutes per game. You play when you need to play, you try to win. It doesn't matter if you go twelve minutes or forty-eight. But that's a lot of minutes. I guess I'm willing to admit that now. It is a lot of minutes. I thought the way I played and practiced, the pressure I put on myself, the way I woke up and went to sleep thinking about how to get better stats, just so I could go outside my house the next day without being yelled at by strangers, was normal at the time. I didn't know any better. I just ran into a wall.

Adding to the darkness was the feeling that I shouldn't be suffering this way at all. I was literally living not only my dream but the dreams of millions of people. I was a professional basketball player with a very lucrative contract. What right did I have to feel anything other than complete satisfaction? Like a lot of athletes and entertainers who came from humble beginnings, I've had a chance to look at it from both sides. Many of us came from $12-per-hour jobs. Many of us used to be broke, used to share a bedroom with multiple family members sleeping on the floor, hoping there was enough money for food or clothes, knowing that sometimes it couldn't be both. That is why we worked so hard in the first place. Sacrificed our bodies, ran the gym until our knees busted and our ligaments tore. Basketball is often for people who have no other choice. If you genuinely have other options, you wouldn't go as far and face as much. You play for fun, but once it gets serious, once it becomes life-or-death, most people will, if they can, find something a little more stable and a little less critical to do with their lives.

The reality is that this system of professional sports is set up to squeeze literally every last thing it can out of the horses. When that much money is at stake, for that many people, your personal health and well-being is going to take a back seat to their bottom line. This is why guys are on the sideline getting pain pills and injections, going to surgeries, getting cartilage and bones and ligaments rebuilt, trying every random, weird, experimental treatment under the sun just to get back out there and play. The human body was not naturally meant to bang up and down a court for eighty-two games. It just wasn't. You have to break yourself in order to do that. You have to, in a sense, break nature.

And that's where, for me, the experience takes on a darker tone. These franchises are worth billions. Your salary may be a lot in the context of what you'd make working at McDonald's, but once you start to think about how much is being made overall, and how small the percentage of that you're seeing is, it feels different. When you stop to think about how you're literally trading your body for cash, not just cash for yourself, but cash to line the pockets of other already wealthy, almost all-white, male owners, when you stop to think about how everything is designed to push you past your physical limits, make you nearly kill yourself, and how the whole time you're getting yelled at by fans, criticized by the press, and booed in your home arena, and you go to sleep and wake up every night aching, you really have to wonder if it's worth it. I'm going to have to have a knee replacement at some point. A hip replacement probably. How much money is your hip worth to you? What is the actual dollar amount you would take if you knew that it would cost you a knee and a hip? It's not as simple a question as it first appears. But the thing was, those difficult moments, those dark nights and painful days, I didn't think I was doing them in exchange for money. I still don't. I was doing them in exchange for playing a sport that I loved. Truly and deeply loved.

While I was struggling with these feelings, I was still doing battle with the sports media. There were times when I didn't really understand or appreciate their agenda. At some point in about 2008, I gave an interview to *Sports Illustrated*. We talked about many things in that interview, and it ended up being about a four-thousand-word piece, but in one small section some comments I made about my teammate Lou Williams were taken entirely out of context by the Philly sports media. I thought the *Sports Illustrated* writer had gotten it right, but in one of those story-about-a-story situations, the local media made it out like I had insulted a teammate and just ran with it. It was hard to understand. And after a while I gave up trying.

Instead, I just started learning how they operate. I started learning how to tell if a reporter is coming with a side angle. You have to pay really close attention to the person asking the question. What do you know about them? What else have they written? How are they looking at you when they ask it? What are the pitfalls you need to be careful of when you're talking? Then you have to make sure not to lose your temper or take it personally. You also need to make sure to keep your answers brief. Because if you get to rambling, you'll start bringing in things that have nothing to do with the conversation, and next thing you know, you're on an entertainment blog with a quote taken all out of context and people calling for you to be suspended. We get criticized for speaking in clichés: "We just wanna go out there and give 110 percent." "We're struggling, and we just need to focus on the game in front of us." And a lot of times that is attributed to what people think is a lack of intellect on our part. But the reality is that we're just trying to make it through the next twenty-four hours without a scandal that causes three million complete strangers to start screaming about how we should be fired. We simply don't have time for it.

If athletes are selfish, it is because there starts to become a point in which you have to be selfish in order to protect yourself. These people are ready to throw your ass under the bus the first chance they get, so why are you about to kill yourself to keep them happy? It's funny. I had an assistant coach at Philly who I won't name but who told me point blank, "Man, you gotta shoot the fucking ball. Stop fucking passing to these dudes. These dudes ain't no good. If you ain't scoring, we ain't gonna win. Stop passing."

This was hard for me to hear. If my teammate is open, I'm going to pass. It's just natural for me. But this guy wouldn't let me stay with that.

"Fuck that, man," he said. "Get your money. Go get your next contract, man. Go get your fucking money. Fuck that passing shit. Man, we ain't winning. Are we going to the playoffs?"

"Hell, yeah, we're going to the playoffs!"

"Alright, maybe we're going to the playoffs. OK. Maybe we might go, but are we going to win the championship? Be fucking realistic."

"No, we're not there yet."

"You're fucking right we ain't there yet. So just shoot the rock and get your money."

I often think of that as the best bad advice anyone ever gave me. Because the truth is, he was looking out for me. He had been in this game a long time and he wanted me to see what he saw. And in some situations, it's not entirely bad advice. If you are a young guy coming up on a team that really isn't there, and you're the only piece your team has, then yes. You kind of have to go get yours. If you want a career in this league, you want to get a decent-size extension, maybe get a trade to a contender, or at least a situation where you aren't entirely responsible for a whole franchise, then yes. You need to put up numbers. You need to keep your stat line in good shape. It's strategic and it's job security.

But it all depends on how you go about it. You can do this in a way that doesn't show disrespect to your teammates. If you're just out there inflating your numbers and your team isn't getting any better, you're not a winner. Simple as that. That's a loser's mentality, and I've always hated that. There are certain guys who are trying to score for their teams. You can tell because they're playing hard on defense. Making that extra dive for the ball, that extra play. Defense doesn't get you shoe contracts or TV commercials. So when a guy is really trying on defense, you know he's really trying for his team.

But you have to be honest. Don't sugarcoat the reality with a lot of junk about dreams and selflessness and teamwork that no one even abides by in the first place. You never know when this thing is going to be over. It's a miracle we're here in the first place. I tell young guys, "Look, get your money while you can. Don't leave nothing on the table."

⸻

Doug Collins was my final coach in Philadelphia. He had come back to the sidelines out of the broadcast booth, and I played under him for the last two years. We made it to the playoffs both times. He had a tremendous grasp of the game and really understood all the movements on a level deeper than other coaches I had known. But he had an Achilles' heel: he wanted to win at any cost. His own background story in the league probably had an impact on how he saw the world. His career was cut short by a rash of injuries to his feet and knees, and of course, he was screwed out of a gold medal in the infamous 1972 Munich Games. The undefeated US team was playing Russia when, late in the game, a "clock malfunction" gave Russia the ball back after the game was effectively over, allowing them three separate tries to get a quick layup and win. The US team declined to take the silver medals, and they were right to do so.

Doug really could have been a Hall of Famer when it was all said and done, but injuries ultimately did him in, and he could never get back to himself. Possibly as a result of this, he had remarkably little tolerance for injuries. You got hurt under Doug and he was basically like, "Fuck that. You gotta play." My own doctor, my trainer, everyone was telling me that I needed rest, that I was playing too many minutes. But Doug was deaf to all that. I played through injuries, he'd say, so you can do the same.

He was really good in the first year, really great at making you buy in. You'd be ready to run through a wall. He used to come to us at the beginning of practice and tell us that Michael Jordan had watched us play the night before. "Dre," he would say, "MJ said way to attack last night. He was impressed." That would fire us up. Wow, Michael Jordan is watching our games! We have to leave it all out there tonight! That really worked until I realized that I had a teammate who knew MJ personally. "Man, MJ ain't watching our games!" he told me. I couldn't believe it. Coach Collins really had me running out there thinking Michael Jordan was tuning in. But that was the Doug Collins genius. He could motivate you like no one else.

But around the second or third year, you begin to pick up on it. You realize that the way he's driving you isn't right. It isn't normal, and teams begin to shift away from him. And if you look at his coaching record, that's what happens. Chicago, Detroit, Washington, Philly—always the same thing. In the third year, things go sideways.

But much of my opinion of Doug Collins is colored by what happened on the last day I spent as a Philadelphia 76er.

It was during the Olympics. One of the most meaningful and special experiences of my life. We were playing for a gold medal, and I was incredibly honored to be there and to be with those guys. I was the seventh man, coming off the bench in London. A nice position to be in. You get good minutes, you get a chance to contribute, and you really feel like that gold medal belongs to you.

We had an off night, and I went to see the US women's soccer team play. I was able to watch the game from a suite with a few people. It was a wonderful game, great view, just overall a very nice vibe. And the women won gold. We were all excited.

Doug was in London as well, calling the games for NBC, so he and I were bumping into each other all over the place. We had even texted earlier that day and he'd told me how excited he was for the next year. Those words exactly. He had texted me, "You played great this year. I can't wait until next year!" The overall vibes were so good that I really appreciated it. It was really the first time in a long time that I felt some level of relief from the situation going on so many miles away back home. My teammate Jrue Holiday was engaged to one of the women's soccer players. I knew he had to be around the stadium somewhere watching the game, so I texted him: "Hey, I'm in a suite, come watch from up here!"

A few minutes later he showed up and we settled in to watch. We were making small talk, but I got the sense he had something on his mind. I thought he was just nervous watching his fiancée play, so I didn't think too much about it. Finally, he came out with it.

"Dude. You getting traded?"

"No, man. I just talked to Doug today. He said everything's cool. Told me he couldn't wait till next year."

A pained look came over Jrue's face. I still didn't realize what was happening.

He handed me his phone. He had been texting with Doug Collins too. "We got a big trade," Doug was saying in his text. "We're going to get Andrew Bynum." I knew what this meant. Bynum was, at that time, a very sought-after player who was commanding a lot of money.

There was no way Philly could have acquired him unless they were moving some other big contracts—unless they were moving me.

That was how I found out. I had played eight years for the franchise. That's 650 games, 24,598 minutes on the floor, 3,468 field goals made from dunks, crashing to the floor for a layup and a foul, driving to the basket at full speed, being known as a player who didn't miss games. Blood on the court, teeth elbowed, eyes poked, fingers stepped on. Countless jerseys sold, millions of fans booing me and cheering me, five coaches, a gaggle of assistants, and no less than three dozen different teammates in and out of those locker rooms, and the way I found out it was finally coming to an end was because a teammate showed me a text message at the Olympics.

It was announced the next day.

I had played for only one team my entire career. It was hard sometimes, it was beautiful sometimes. The fans and press in Philadelphia are like the fans and press nowhere else. And that's a good thing. None of us could stand it if the whole country was like that. I got to learn so much from the men I played with and under there. And I would never, ever trade a moment of that time for anything. It made me grow up, it taught me how to take care of my career and how to take care of myself. I will always be grateful for Philadelphia.

A lot about that experience was great, and a lot was painful. But no matter how bad it got, there would always be something to remind you that you can't take any of this too seriously. One game, I was warming up, stretching on the floor during the pregame, and a player from the other team came over to me. This was a guy I had known for years. He was a great character and a great player. Maybe even a Hall of Famer one day. Time will tell. Anyway, this was toward the end of the season, when the playoff seedings had long been decided, and what we were about to embark on was, essentially, a meaningless game. Situations like this can be hard. You're either exhausted and wishing you could rest up for the playoffs or you're already thinking about where you're going to play golf in the off-season. The main thing you don't want is anyone to get hurt in a game like this. You want everyone to keep it cool. But sometimes you get a rookie or two in there playing hard, trying to show their worth off the bench, and now all of a sudden guys are banging around for no reason at all. You wish you could skip a game like this, but the tickets have been sold. You have to play. I reached out my hand to dap this guy up and he didn't take it. Instead he leaned in real close to me, opened his mouth, and exhaled into my nostrils so I could smell his breath. He smelled, honestly, like an entire frat party had taken place in his mouth.

"What the fuck?" I said, laughing.

"Yo, I'm drunk as fuck right now."

I couldn't believe it. This dude was wasted. All I could think of was that I was going to have a good game whenever I ended up guarding him, because we were going to win this one going away.

Tip-off happened and it was a different story entirely. This man turned into Drunken Master. As good as he was sober, he was ridiculous this night. He was lighting the floor entirely up, knocking in threes, scoring from every single direction. Shaking, baking, dunking, really kind of making us look stupid. He torched us plain and simple. I know he's never done anything like that before or since, but if I played that well drunk, I don't know if I'd ever stop. I still laugh when I think about that. Sometimes basketball is a real headache. But after it's all said and done, it's still just a game.

06

Elevation

n Denver the sun is so bright that on some mornings I would see two or three feet of snow on my way to practice, but by noon, not only would it be gone, but the ground would be bone-dry, as if it had never been there in the first place. And this was exactly what I needed after my increasingly claustrophobic experiences in Philadelphia. This was a place where people were in a more relaxed mood. It was insanely clean and outdoorsy. The fans cared but they weren't aggravated or negative after a loss. They just, you know, *rooted for the home team*, which was a concept that I had forgotten even existed.

When I arrived at the practice facility for the first day, I was amazed. Because they had one. I had gotten so used to the cramped basement facility in Philadelphia that I was genuinely blown away to walk into the situation they had in Denver. Here were brand-new weight machines, massage tables, catered meals. It was a completely different vibe. My first practice was filled with hopefulness about what we could accomplish. Not just because we were such a good team, but because everything to me felt like a fresh start.

I didn't know yet how good we could or couldn't be, although I was familiar with most players on that team and tight with a few of them from basketball circles, including our point guard Ty Lawson. An incredibly bright player who came out of UNC, Ty was part of the ever-shrinking number of true point guards in the league. He had come up under the tutelage of Chauncey Billups and Andre Miller, a guy I played with in Philadelphia, and like his mentors was a passer first and would score only when he felt like he had no other choice. I can still see him bringing the ball up court, scanning left and right, calling out plays. It felt good to be in hands like that, to be on the floor with a guy you knew was primarily concerned with watching the play develop and making sure that everyone got to their spots.

On our first day of practice, he and I got to talking.

"Damn, Dre," he said. "I'm glad you're finally here because I was getting sick of hearing them talk about you."

"What do you mean?"

"Well, all last year, all I heard from the coaching staff was 'When we get Andre . . . when Andre comes.' They've been obsessed with bringing you in here and I'm glad it's finally happened."

That made me feel good, to know that I wasn't an afterthought or a burden, or someone the fans loved, then hated, then loved. It began to occur to me that I hadn't really felt trustful of the office in Philadelphia. I wasn't always sure that they had my back. Just the mere notion of that being different here totally threw into stark relief just how difficult some aspects of my time in Philly had been.

Fittingly, our first game of the season was against none other than the Philadelphia 76ers. I expected them to boo me when my name was announced, and I was not disappointed. As soon as the announcer said my height, the capacity crowd exploded into a chorus of jeers. I couldn't even hear my name called. They were booing me like I had personally kicked each of their puppies. I tried not to be rattled, but there was a lot of emotion for me in that game.

Why were they booing me? It wasn't as if I was the one who requested a trade. I played there for eight years and had to face trade rumors pretty much nonstop. I would have gladly come back, but instead I was lied to by my own coach. Yet I was the one they were booing? I caught a glimpse of Doug Collins standing on the sideline, himself looking a little apprehensive. He had a lot on the line here too. If I were to come out and put up 35 on them, then he would look like a fool for trading me.

The wounds for everyone were still fresh. Right from the opening tip I was determined to make an impact, to show them what a mistake they had made in treating me as they did. We won the tip and my first bucket was a step-back mid-range jumper on an assist from Ty. Boom. The crowd booed some more. I tried to put it out of my head. They missed a jumper on the other end, Jordan Hamilton grabbed the board, and soon the ball was in my hands at the corner. I heaved up a three and missed. Badly. Things started to unravel from that point on. I could feel that I was pressing hard, but I couldn't control it. I missed a six-foot jumper later, and soon after that turned the ball over on a Jason Richardson steal. The crowd loved that. I was able to get a steal and a dunk off of Lavoy Allen later in the first period, and a few other halfway decent plays, but most of the game I felt like I was trying to push twenty different boulders uphill at the same time. I couldn't get a rhythm, I was missing reads, committing turnovers, and nothing was coming easy. It was one of the worst games I played. The more I struggled, the more I pushed. And the more I pushed, the worse I played. When the buzzer sounded, we had lost 75–84. I went 5 for 13 from the field, committed 4 turnovers and only scored 11 points. Doug Collins walked off the court with a smile on his face. I did not.

I was living in a little apartment downtown. I had brought one cousin with me for company and to help with running business-related stuff, and I began to feel for him. He was bored to tears. There seemed to be almost no black people in Denver, no nightlife that we really felt drawn to. For my cousin, that was hard, but for me it was perfect. I loved being able to walk to practice or to games in the crisp, cool Denver air. Just like those few weeks in Chicago when I was preparing for the draft, I was once again treated to a life with a completely single-minded purpose. I had my apartment. I had the sandwich shop that I liked to walk to. And I finally had a practice facility that I could go to anytime of the day or night.

And that's what I did. Sleep continued to be a problem for me, as it was at Arizona, and as it was in Philly. It had gotten better, but there were still occasional nights that would turn into morning right before my bleary eyes. Having access to the practice facility and weight room at all times helped me tremendously. I would sometimes go late at night, lift and shoot, lift and shoot. Even though it would have been better to be sleeping, the solitude was nice. But better still was that I was beginning to learn how to channel my attention, to put my sometimes overly active brain toward something useful. In Philly, the obsession was damaging because it was entirely about proving media wrong. I was motivated by resentment, by frustration. There is a self-destructive aspect to that. It almost felt like, "Fine, you want me to kill myself? Watch me kill myself." But in Denver that element was almost entirely gone. The fans there were just content to have a winning team.

Our weight trainer in Denver was a genuinely unbelievable person. And what I mean by that is I literally could not believe this guy when I first saw him. His name was Steve Hess. He stood about five foot five and was about as thick with muscle as he was tall. A well-tanned, middle-age white dude with graying dreads pulled back into an ever-present ponytail, he spoke with a thick, raspy voice in what I would later learn was a New Zealand accent. But the thing that I really couldn't believe about him was how incredibly positive he was. He was happy and ready to work every single day. Whether he was working one-on-one with me or managing half the squad in the weight room, his enthusiasm was infectious. Every sentence he delivered was rapid-fire encouragement mixed with wisdom. "That's how you do it, Andre. Always pay attention and attention pays off." I had never seen such spirit combined with such specificity. I have met a lot of athletic trainers who speak in platitudes, who are always saying stuff about pushing yourself and getting better, but Steve showed me what the difference was when you really 100 percent believed in a guy. We believed in him, and he believed in us.

During times that may have otherwise been difficult, Steve's steady, almost hilariously cheery encouragement kept me afloat and started to slowly have an effect on me. I began to see my body as something that had limitations and needed to be treated as such. "People have this misconception that because they're professional athletes," Steve once said, "their bodies adhere differently. But here's the thing. They're still human bodies. They go through a ton of stress. So if you're not appropriate in every aspect of it, they're still gonna break down." That was the kind of attitude that pushed my training and game to the next level. It was intentional but gentle. In Philadelphia, I had thought that all I needed was more will, more pushing, more determination. I had thought that the cost of it didn't matter. But working with Steve, I began to see things more holistically. I could not push myself against my body. I had to align my will and the will of my body into one seamless machine.

We tried to bounce back from that awful first game in Philly, but twenty-two of our first thirty-two contests were on the road and the season began with a very middling 17-15 record. It was not looking good on paper, but I could see that we were feeling each other out. Danilo Gallinari was the big name on that team, and he was a lot of what he was cracked up to be. I really liked his game. He was incredibly versatile and a sneaky-hard worker. He was relentless on the boards, a truly gifted shooter, and, having come from the European game, where there was such emphasis on X's and O's, he—like Ty Lawson—had a real IQ on the floor.

I remember a game not too long after Christmas 2012 when we played the Dallas Mavericks. Danilo started off kind of cold in that game, if I recall correctly. A few misses, a few turnovers. Dallas wasn't known as an especially defensive team, but they were making some nice, disciplined switches on us in the first half. This was around the point in the season, three or so months in, when teams were starting to have to decide who was the guy they were going to have to shut down. Was it me or was it Danilo? You could feel teams trying different approaches to us defensively—sometimes a double-team, sometimes a switch—and that's how you knew they were struggling to handle the one-two punch we presented. It gave us confidence.

Right at the end of the first half of that game, Danilo drained a big three. On the ensuing play, Andre Miller stole the ball on a bad pass inbound from Vince Carter and kicked it to Ty Lawson, who tried a last-second three. Ty missed, but Danilo came crashing in for a putback dunk literally right at the buzzer. It was so close they had to review it to make sure it was good. From that point on, I was just so hyped for the kid—I guess I was really feeling the experience of being a part of this new team—that I started hyping him up at half-time and continued into the third quarter. I was cheering for him crazy and I could see it was getting to him. Every time he made a shot and I was on the bench, I'd be the one jumping up the highest and yelling the loudest. "Man, bust they fuckin' ass!!!" He was trying to keep from smiling, but he was having a hard time playing it cool. I guess they don't do it like that in Europe, because he was looking at me like he had never had a teammate cheer for him like that. He ended that game with 39 points, including seven threes on 63 percent shooting from beyond the arc. Things like that strengthened the bond between us. They made the vibe workable even though we weren't really a "tight-knit" team. I barely ever saw Danilo off the court. But I was learning that if a team doesn't hang tough off the court, then part of my job was to help us have the chemistry we needed on the court.

I was close to a handful of players from that squad though. Corey Brewer was a guy I would hang out with off court, as was Ty Lawson. But one of the teammates I connected with most was Wilson Chandler. To this day, he is one of the men I respect most in the league. Wilson is a very quiet man. Unassuming, but smart. And like most of the players I gravitate toward, Wilson is a thinker. He and I would occasionally talk after games until late into the night. Sometimes about politics, sometimes about the game or about the business of the game. But it was often about spirituality. He was always searching for answers to the bigger questions. What is our purpose? What can we do with our positions of power? What is real power?

As basketball players, we find ourselves in this complicated position. We are extremely fortunate to be able to earn a living doing something we love. We are granted something of an exalted status because of the fact that we're on TV, and in this country, we believe that anyone on TV is somehow special. And we earn money. In some cases, lots of it. For most of us, this grants access and gifts a thousand times more extravagant than we had growing up in our neighborhoods.

As Americans, we are led to believe that this in and of itself should be the path toward complete satisfaction. If we make enough money, have enough success, then we should be free from all struggles—or more accurately, our struggles are no longer valid. But what most of us find after a while, and much to our surprise, is that even with all the cash and prizes, the question of purpose remains. Pain and suffering still remain. Anger and frustration still remain. It would seem that most people who gain some measure of what we think of as material success have experienced this truth, but the effect is amplified for black people. Because of our shared destiny, it is not possible for one of us to be completely free and happy while our collective people are subject to violence, oppression, and dehumanization. Or rather, the only way for such a thing to be possible is if that person makes a conscious decision to turn their back entirely on their people. And that cannot be me. I have always had a sense of race consciousness. It came first from growing up in a place where racial violence was literally in the DNA of the town, and it continued as I sought out learning and education in high school and college. My talks with Salim Stoudamire at Arizona and Chris Webber and Elton Brand in Philly gave me further motivation to seek knowledge and understanding of history, politics, and finance. But in Denver a new thing was happening, especially through those conversations with Wilson Chandler. It was a next-leveling of my consciousness. I was just beginning to understand how spiritual fitness was intertwined with everything. I was becoming aware of a new kind of discipline, an internal mental and emotional clarity that was, on the one hand, an extension of what I'd learned in

all the years of working out and pushing myself, but also was something wholly different. I wasn't learning it yet. I was just learning that
it existed and that I could be rising toward it.

———————

As the season wore on, we became a more cohesive unit on the floor
and were able to put together a number of win streaks that made us
feel as though we just might be able to do something special this year.
Denver had never won a championship, nor had the team ever even
been to the finals. I wasn't foolish enough to think I was going to change
that in one season, but it was clear that we were hooping at a nice level
and I enjoyed that feeling. George Karl, the coach, was a man who
knew basketball inside and out from an X's and O's perspective. While
my relationship with him was not what you would call close, we had an
understanding: we would help each other win because it was mutually
beneficial for us to do so. Karl, I think, could see that I knew the game,
could help keep guys on track mentally, and, if necessary, could be a
leading or second-leading scorer. I could see that he knew how to
scheme for teams and how to put us in the best position to win.

Karl was my sixth NBA coach, and I was beginning to understand
something new about the breed. Many of them had egos just like
many players did. I don't know why this surprised me, but I suppose
that on some level I, like everyone else, had bought into the inherent
hierarchy of the league more than I realized. People like to think of
coaches as somehow all-around more capable and better people than
players. It is assumed that they know more about basketball, which is
true. And it is assumed that they have increased life experience,
which is also, in many cases, true. But underlying that are a set of
unspoken assumptions about their actual worth as people. You hear

about coaches having to "get their teams under control." They are to be respected at all times no matter what they say or do. If you disparage a coach in the press, everyone talks about you as the locker room cancer. Rarely do you hear about a coach being a locker room cancer. But why is it more likely for a player to be a disruption than a coach with an oversize ego? In fact, can't a coach do more damage because the structure allows him more power? Can't a coach be wrong? Most people have to work much harder to see it that way. I got along perfectly fine with Coach Karl because our team played well and we needed something from each other. But I couldn't help noticing that he was quick to take credit when things went well but slow to take blame when they didn't.

Later, players began to speak out more honestly about their experiences with George Karl after he published a book with unflattering things to say about many of them, especially after he took a particularly nasty shot at Kenyon Martin for not growing up with a father in his life. It smacked of everything that was wrong with some coaches: narrow-mindedness, smugness, and a feeling of superiority. If you are a white man whose job is to boss black men around, this is not a great look for you. Karl's legacy was particularly tarnished by what he said in that book, and I do feel that sometimes, in the end, people get what they deserve.

Just as my time in Denver was opening me up to new self-understanding, it was also opening me up to a deeper understanding of the business of basketball. Denver was a small-market team and the economics of that situation are entirely different from those of a team in New York or Los Angeles. Or even Philadelphia. The most obvious thing is that it's entirely disadvantageous for a team like Denver to ever go over the salary cap. To enforce parity in the league, the NBA has determined that the collective salary of a team cannot go over a certain number. This is to prevent big-market teams, or teams with insanely rich owners, from simply buying up all the talent and winning every year. But there's another level to it. A team is allowed to go over the cap, but if they do so, they must pay a penalty, called a luxury tax, that is redistributed to the rest of the teams. The problem is that a lot of teams are willing to pay that tax because, again, the barrier is still money. So it's sort of like saying that if you're rich, you can't spend more money than the poor do, but if you want to spend more money, you just have to spend more money.

Bigger market teams can do this and still remain in the black because they have the fan base and broadcast deals to generate the revenue to cover it. But for a mid-market team like Denver, the luxury tax hits heavier. They weren't even selling out playoff games. So if you're the Nuggets franchise, it doesn't make financial sense to break open the bank in order to win, even if you have wealthy ownership, which they did. In small markets, you can either put winning first or financial gain first, but rarely can you do both. What you hope happens is that you can catch lightning in a bottle by building through the draft and lucking out on a free agent or two. You hope to assemble a team of relatively low-salary players who somehow come together to make a dent.

I began to wonder if we had that. Denver had decided to bring me in on a contract year, which was smart on their part. Most players are a little more focused during a contract year. It's only human, and normal—no different from how a student puts in extra hours when studying for a final. It's exam time and grades are coming out. So even if you were already a good student, you're going to go a little harder leading up to test week. Nonetheless, I made sure that I put in max effort all the time.

I was starting to have a pretty statistically solid year because of this, and by January 2013 we were beginning to put together some wins. I had thought that the chemistry might shift in a positive direction after Gallinari's big game, and I was right. We had a nice home stand where we took six in a row in January, lost two, and then won another nine straight, including an overtime victory against Kevin Durant, Russell Westbrook, and the Oklahoma City Thunder. Westbrook hit a twenty-seven-footer to tie that game and send it into overtime, but Andre Miller and the Manimal, Kenneth Faried, were balling big-time in the extra period, and we walked away with the win.

When we came back from the All-Star break, we were pumped. We picked up where we left off and ultimately went on a fifteen-game win streak in the last week of February and into March. My numbers were getting even better, as I had really found myself within the flow of Karl's offense. There was a buzz around the league about us. Were we for real? We certainly thought so. We managed to lock down the number-three seed in the playoffs, and toward the end of that season we felt that we had peaked at the right time. We had been an entirely different team after All-Star break. We had gone 24-4 since coming back and we were en route to the single best season in franchise history. And as far as we were concerned, we were just getting started.

Then April 4, 2013, happened.

In the seventy-sixth game of an eighty-two-game season, a game that meant almost nothing, Danilo Gallinari tore his ACL in a freak play. I couldn't believe it. None of us could. He was driving to the basket, the defender stepped out to make him change direction—no contact—and somehow Danilo just landed wrong on his left foot and went down. You could tell right away that it was serious. The mood in the locker room that game was like nothing I've ever experienced. We were a good team, we had overachieved and played our hearts out, and here, for no comprehensible reason, we had lost one of our most valuable players.

We faced Golden State in the first round. They were the number-six seed that year, a team that was still up-and-coming under Mark Jackson. They were not where they would ultimately be, of course, but they had Steph and Klay as a rapidly developing nucleus. And their coach knew it. That was the year Mark Jackson caught flak for saying, "In my opinion they're the greatest shooting backcourt in the history of the game." Reporters scoffed, fans laughed, and Jackson was roundly ridiculed. But as players, we took note of that. Jackson knew his NBA history, and that's not something a guy like him just says without careful consideration. But more than that, it spoke to how much Mark stood behind his guys. The fact that he was willing to make such a bold statement, to potentially take such heat for his players—there were not a lot of other coaches I could think of who seemed that devoted to the men on their team.

We competed. We really did, but it was Steph Curry's coming-out party. He was shooting at a very high level, and without Gallinari, we simply did not have the firepower to answer their scoring. It was like no matter what we did, they could do it better. We scored 108, they scored 110. We got 111, they got 115. Game 2 was an absolute shoot-out—we gave them 117 points and were balling on all cylinders. They scored 131 that night. And Steph and Klay went the whole game without shooting *one free throw*. We were outgunned. We lost that series 4–2. We never stood a chance.

That was the unfortunate end of something that could have been much bigger. We had won fifty-seven regular season games, the most for a Nuggets team since they joined the NBA in 1976. We may have been the best squad in the team's fifty-one seasons, and that meant something to me. And I had put up some of the best playoff numbers of my whole career: 18 points per game, 8 rebounds, 5.3 assists, and 2 steals. But going into the off-season, which, for me, meant unrestricted free agency, I had to look at the situation. I was twenty-nine years old and about to start my tenth NBA season. And I hadn't even sniffed an NBA Finals appearance. I liked playing in Denver, but I was not bullish on our prospects for the long term. I had learned to look at the bigger picture for the franchise. I knew everyone's salary, and I knew that I had put up good numbers, and I felt, after having hung around there for a year, that I had a good sense of the team's financial limitations. If they were to somehow re-sign me on a new contract, who else would they be able to bring in? Who else were they going to be able to keep? It was a good team, but where were we going to go from here? Especially in the West with the Spurs still dominating, Oklahoma looking strong despite having lost James Harden, and Golden State clearly on the come-up? Let's not forget that in 2013, the Memphis Grizzlies, with Marc Gasol and Zach Randolph, were still factored heavily into every postseason conversation.

I was going to have to test the market to see what I could get elsewhere. There were teams that wanted me, I was sure of it, and there were teams I wanted.

I found myself, toward the end of that year, thinking more and more about that season opener against Philadelphia. I had noticed something about myself, about that game that night, but I hadn't put my finger on exactly what it was. What had happened? I had been knocked off my game by something inside me. Was it because I wasn't playing within the flow of the game? I was trying to win, to prove a point. The Philly fans, Doug Collins, the unfairness of it all had gotten in my head somehow. I thought back to my earlier lessons, the times I stepped on the court at a high school tournament, banging around with guys I was convinced were better than me. I remembered how I had tried to prove myself, how I had been unsure, and how that had made my game stagnant and slow. But I also remembered games where I had just hooped. The scrimmage at Arizona. The game me and Rich McBride played against the Illinois squad when we were in high school. I had experienced a kind of freedom in those games. A simplicity. I had just hooped.

There is a difference between playing basketball and hooping. Hooping is free and simple. The work that goes into it is complicated and intense, but in the actual moments of play, there is some kind of, I didn't know the word for it yet, but there was something there. A lightness. An elevation. Steve Hess had shown me that this was possible. Wilson Chandler had shown me that there was a spirituality to be pursued in all aspects of my life. My last few years in Philadelphia had been, at times, a nightmare of self-consciousness and self-doubt. In Denver I had tiny little moments of awakening, but as a team we were not good enough to play deep into the postseason, which I felt I needed to do. I had a very strong sense that the next contract I signed was going to be my last contract. I already had ten years in this league, and even that achievement was against all odds. I was playing with house money at this point, and I didn't want my next experience to be darkened by all the things I had learned could be unpleasant about the game. I wanted to win, sure, but I wanted more than that. I wanted to hoop. Once again, it was time to search elsewhere for what I needed.

07

Find the Flow

No one likes it when you say that unrestricted free agency is like the shackles being off, but that's always the image that comes to mind for me. No team owns you anymore. In restricted free agency, you can still talk to other teams, but your team has the right of first refusal. They can retain you if they feel like it by simply matching the offer any other team makes to you. But in unrestricted free agency, you can go anywhere you want.

Every time I think of free agency I have to think about Curt Flood, the black baseball player and two-time All-Star who sacrificed his entire career so that players like me could have some say over where we played. At the time he played, Major League Baseball had what was called a reserve clause, which meant that a team that drafted a player owned him for his entire career, even after his contract had expired, and could therefore dictate trades at whim with no input from the player. Flood was traded from St. Louis to Philadelphia in 1963 but refused to go because he felt that (*a*) the team sucked, and (*b*) the fans were racist. He wrote a letter to the commissioner of baseball challenging the fact that he could be traded to whomever, whenever, even though he was no longer under contract.

"After twelve years in the major leagues, I do not feel I am a piece of property to be bought and sold irrespective of my wishes," Flood said in a 1969 letter. "I believe that any system which produces that result violates my basic rights as a citizen and is inconsistent with the laws of the United States and of the several States." He went on to suggest, shockingly, that he believed that he had a right to consider offers from other teams before making a decision, an idea that was nearly unheard of at the time.

Flood sued Major League Baseball, arguing that the reserve clause was essentially indentured servitude and violated antitrust laws, and the case went all the way to the Supreme Court in 1972. His side lost 5–3 (one justice had to recuse himself because he had an ownership stake in Anheuser-Busch, which owned the Cardinals), and Flood was essentially blackballed from the sport. His teammates said that he received four or five death threats a day from fans who accused him of trying to destroy the game. He played only thirteen more games in his career after refusing to report to Philadelphia, but his argument had made an impact. In 1975, MLB contract arbitrator Peter Seitz ruled that two pitchers who had played a year without a contract should actually be allowed to become free agents, essentially setting the precedent for nullification of the reserve clause and starting widespread free agency.

Because of Curt Flood and his sacrifices, it is now commonly accepted that players should have a say in their own place of employment. And I feel like that's something none of us should ever forget.

The year my free agency hit, 2012, was a bizarre year in that regard. In any off-season you typically have the first-tier guys, the most sought after, whose decisions will impact the way the rest of the period shakes out. That year, Dwight Howard was the big name. So I really couldn't make a decision until he did, because it would be a domino effect. Meanwhile, July 1 came, which was the official opening of the free-agency period, and I had back-to-back meetings scheduled at my agent's office in LA with Dallas, New Orleans, Denver, Detroit, and Golden State that morning. My first meeting was with Sacramento, which made an offer in the first five minutes. They didn't want to waste time and they didn't want me meeting with anyone else. They made it abundantly clear that they wanted me badly. It felt nice, but they were asking me to commit to them five minutes after free agency started, which was simply not possible. "I appreciate your excitement," I told them, "but I have to explore my options." They reluctantly gave me until midnight that night to make the call, but that, too, didn't sit well with me. I knew that with so many moving parts around the league, things could take much longer than that to reveal themselves. I told them thanks but no thanks. It was the biggest offer I'd had in free agency up until that point in my career, but I simply couldn't commit to it without knowing what other situations were realistically on the table.

When the Warriors came in, they had Mark Jackson, General Manager Bob Myers, owner Joe Lacob and his son Kirk Lacob, and a few other suits. I didn't think it was necessary to waste time with a lot of glad-handing and smoke blowing. This was my first-choice team, and there was no real advantage to playing coy about that. I wasn't trying to get the most money; I was trying to land in the best situation for me as a player. "You guys don't have to give me a whole spiel," I said. "I already know what it is. Let's see if we can figure out a way to get this done. If we can't, I still respect you and the organization. But I'm interested in the culture, and I'm interested in playing for Coach Jackson, in the way he coaches the game."

I had seen something really important in that series against Golden State. His players were playing with confidence, and that's a lot rarer than you would think. I've had coaches in the past who would let every player go, and the result was a disaster. I've had others who would suffocate you, hang on your every play, and tell you that you were doing everything wrong with such regularity that you could no longer stay in the flow of the game when the ball was in your hands. But when I watched Coach Jackson, I could tell that he had the perfect balance. He would encourage players to find whatever was naturally occurring within their game and then he would let them loose to do it as much as they wanted. Which meant that, playing under him, everyone looked as good as they possibly could. He got guys paid. One of his favorite sayings was "If I don't get you paid here, I'm going to get you paid somewhere." On the one hand, it was about the money—I mean, who doesn't want to hear that? But on the other hand, it was something deeper. There was a psychological benefit to a coach who saw you as an adult professional and who prioritized helping you along with your career above all else. It was respect. Respect as a human, respect as an adult, respect as a professional. Mark Jackson had that and it made you not only play better but feel better.

Nonetheless, the Warriors were direct too. They were flattered that I was so upfront and motivated to come aboard, but they were also surprised. They simply didn't have the cap space to make my number work. They would certainly see what they could do, but from their point of view, it was going to be hard. I left that meeting feeling that Golden State wasn't going to happen, which made Dallas the front-runner. My agent, Rob, and Mavericks owner Mark Cuban worked out a number, and by the end of the week, I was beginning to look at places to rent in the Dallas–Fort Worth area. There was just one hitch. The deal was *almost* as good as done, but they would have to wait for final word about where Dwight Howard would end up, because that would impact the movement of money and players all over the league. If he went to this team, then this team could trade this guy, which meant that team could free up space for this move, etc. All of free agency hinged on him. Dwight was supposed to make his decision by that Friday, which was July 5. So that's when I would know if Dallas was happening.

Friday came and went, and Dwight still had not signed anywhere. He announced that he would need the weekend to think about it, and that he'd announce on Monday and we should all just sit tight. This meant that a whole bunch of players would have to wait until Monday, July 8, to find out where were going to end up. Meanwhile, I was just wasting time in LA, bored and antsy, waiting for this whole thing to be resolved. So that weekend I did what I always do when I'm agitated. I went to the gym. My old Philly teammate Evan Turner was in town, so I called him up to see if he wanted to work out while we waited to know what our futures were going to be. He, as always, was down, and by Monday morning, 8:00 a.m., Evan and I were at the gym getting it in.

We stopped for breakfast after the workout and my phone rang. It was Rob. Dwight's indecision had had the unexpected effect of giving the Golden State front office extra time to move things around. Rather than acquiring me outright on top of their current contracts, which they could not afford to do without going over the cap, they had been able to work out a sign-and-trade with Denver. The Nuggets had come to accept the fact that I was not coming back, but losing me flat-out in free agency meant they would get nothing in return. Now, with a sign-and-trade, they could re-sign me and trade me immediately to Golden State in exchange for players. For Golden State's part, this meant that in the trade they would be getting contracts off the books to make room for me. It was a win for me and for the Warriors, and for Denver it was the second-best scenario after signing me outright.

The same day I spoke to one of the Denver executives in LA. He was upset about how things had shaken out, and he was not hiding it. "You took less money to go with another team?" he said to me. Technically that was true. Golden State had given me four years at $48 million, whereas Denver had offered five years at something like $57 million. But that fifth year in Denver was going to be a partial guarantee, which meant they could cut me or get rid of me at any point. I tried to imagine myself fifteen years into my career playing for a middling team that could just bounce me halfway through the season or whenever they felt like it, and it did not put me in the mood to sign a contract. I tried to explain that it wasn't about the money. It was about the basketball. I saw the moves they were making, and those moves weren't inspiring me with confidence. I wanted to play somewhere where I was on board with the team philosophy and where I could see us trending upward. I wanted to go work where I was happy to go work. Wasn't that my right? Wasn't that what Curt Flood had sacrificed his career for?

There was no outright hostility, but I definitely noticed a cooling in my relationship with several members of the Denver front office after the events of that summer. I would, as always, see them at weddings, conferences, and charity events. And the interactions were different. Before, it would have been a hug and a long conversation. Now, it was a head nod and them turning back to their drinks. I wish I could say it surprised me but it didn't. My entire time in Philly I had been subject to trade rumors. I'd wake up in the morning and hear on the radio on the way to practice that my team was looking to get rid of me. "It's just business," I was always told. "It's nothing personal, you understand." And I did. But that summer I found myself wondering how it was that when a team wanted to change players, it was just business, but when players wanted to change teams, it was an insult.

I arrived in the Bay Area about a month or so before training camp so I could play pickup with the guys every day. This was Mark's vision. Just letting guys hoop and get to know each other in a relaxed environment. Or I should say somewhat relaxed. Harrison Barnes was trying to kill me. He had elbows in my chest, fighting for possessions. He was on only his second year at that point, but I had come in at his position, so he could see the writing on the wall, and he wasn't going to go down without a fight. But that excited me. It was good to see that guys weren't just rolling over. They were fighting to be on this team. He's since become one of my closest friends in the league.

By the time we got to training camp, I had a good sense of this squad, and it was even better up close than I had thought. The vibe was a unique combination of relaxed and serious. You might call it "professional." About a week into camp I had a moment that I'll always remember as my introduction to the team. We were going through a drill, something simple. I don't remember exactly what it was. And Pete Myers, an assistant coach at the time, just came at me, yelling. "Iguodala! What are you doing? That's not how you do it! *This* is what you do!" I was taken aback. I hadn't had a coach unload on me like that in a long time. I was supposed to be the big get for this off-season, and here was this guy screaming on me like I was a rookie.

And I loved it. It gave me tremendous respect for the squad. It showed me that everyone on that team was getting held to the same standard, no matter who they were. That's when it clicked for me that this team had what it took to make something next level. Typically you notice on teams that every player is treated slightly differently based on the size of their contracts, and while that makes a certain kind of sense, I think it subconsciously communicates that the team philosophy isn't the most important thing. The player's egos are. Here was something different. Here was an opportunity to build as a basketball player and grow as a student of the game.

That was just one of the things I would come to love about playing in the Bay Area. The whole experience was new to me, because most players don't even know that Oracle Arena is in Oakland. When you're a visiting team, you fly into San Francisco, you stay in San Francisco, and you practice in San Francisco. Then you take a bus across the bridge to Oakland, but by that time you're so focused on preparing for the game that you don't really notice that you're changing cities. You might schedule a tour to Alcatraz or something like that if you have time, but as a visitor you don't really experience a lot of Oakland. But as a Warrior, it's entirely different. Oracle becomes your home.

There are only a few arenas in the country like it. Most cities you play in, the arena is big multiuse building, and it feels like it. In Chicago, the United Center is a huge, cavernous building. The arena is cold because often you're overlapping with hockey season. Wells Fargo Center in Philadelphia and American Airlines Arena in Miami are both enormous. Staples Center in Los Angeles is basically an entertainment center. These places feel like concert halls where you just happen to be playing a game of basketball. But there are a few places around the country that feel like gymnasiums, like buildings built entirely for basketball. Portland, Indiana, Madison Square Garden—these are places where the crowd is loud and right up on you, almost like in a high school or college game. And that energy is electric. Certain arenas just have an aura to them. It's like the building is somehow able to catch and focus the energy of all twenty thousand people right onto the floor. Oracle is one of those places.

Even playing there as a visitor, there was always something special about playing at Oracle. No matter how good that year's team was, the building always felt like it was sold out. It could be game sixty-five of a 28-37 season, and the fans would be chanting like it was game 7 of the conference finals. And there was a specific chant that the fans would do: "WAAAAAARRRIOORS . . . WAAAAAAAARRRIOOORRS!" It was a long, hollow, haunting chant, swelling up from the seats, filling up the ceiling, and raining down on you like an echo. It sounded like someone was coming for you in the dead of night. I loved it. It got me fired up. They would even do it during warm-ups. It's easily the best fan chant in all the NBA. Once you heard that, even as a visitor, you got hyped. You would get chills. You wanted to have a good game just to respect the fans for the energy they were bringing.

And the fans knew basketball. You often hear about whether fan bases are smart, and there's something to that. Warriors fans, especially in those Don Nelson and Mark Jackson years, really knew the game. They would react to referee calls the instant they were made. In some arenas the fans don't know what's happening until it's replayed on the jumbotron, but Warriors fans were kind of like New York or Indiana fans that way. They reacted right away. You'd hear them cheering a crossover or a nice crisp pass even while the play was still happening. Sometimes with fans of bigger, flashier teams, it feels like they're not at the game to watch basketball, but just to be seen. They might as well be at the club. But whenever you played a game in Oakland, those fans were there because they loved the sport and they wanted to see it played at a high level.

And when I became a player there, that respect for the game was everywhere. Not just in the building, but in the organization, and especially in the coaching. It was like a kind of faith, a very fundamental belief that by truly focusing on the game, on executing it at a high level, on treating each player as an adult and as a professional, then the rest would take care of itself. The organization embodied that and so did Mark Jackson. He was honest but incredibly support-ive. Sometimes during the season, I would pass up a shot and Mark would pull me aside and give it to me straight. "C'mon, man," he'd say. "I can't have you out there passing up shots. I can't have you out there not attacking. Do *you*. You attack, you play defense, so go do *you*!" That kind of attitude empowered us and gave us confidence. To this day I contend that Steph and Klay would never have turned into the Steph and Klay who set record books on fire if it weren't for this attitude by Mark Jackson. Encourage you where your game is strong, correct you plainly where you need correcting. He was calling those guys the greatest shooting backcourt of all time before most fans had ever heard their names. And he was giving them a vision of them-selves that they could see but no one else could. He was validating their best versions of themselves.

I remember once in a meeting, he told Steph, "I don't care how many turnovers you got. People are always talking about turnovers, but I don't care how many you make. In my opinion, you're the best point guard in the league. You're the All-Star. This is your team, so do what you want with it." It meant something because he said that in front of the whole team. He didn't pull him to the side and gas him up like some coaches would do. He staked his idea in the ground in front of us. He believed in Stephen Curry and that was what we were going to do as a team. "If a point guard goes at you, Steph," he said one time, "you have my permission to go back at him. I'll take the loss." Most guys would be hating in a situation like this: "Man, look at this dude. Coach gonna keep letting this dude do whatever?" But in my mind that was an amazing feeling to give to your point guard.

It was a good year overall, even though Coach Jackson had what turned out to be a chaotic relationship with the organization. I don't know all of what happened there, but I know that for many of us, it was an uncomfortable situation. We really liked Coach, and the organization had been good too. So we didn't know what to think. When it came down to it, we wanted to support Mark because he was the guy who had, on a day-in-and-day-out basis, supported us. So in the media we made it clear. We support our coach.

As the season wore on, injuries made their mark on our season. Early in the year, I had missed a string of games with a hamstring injury. Andrew Bogut ended up missing the playoffs with a rib injury. This was a problem because our bench that year wasn't very deep. If you notice, this team has only lost two rounds in the playoffs since I came, and both times Bogut was injured. He played a much more pivotal role than most people gave him credit for.

Coach had created something really special with the roster he had. He had installed an unprecedented combination of defensive intensity and offensive freedom. But in the end, it was not enough. Bogut's injury in the playoffs that year meant that we did not have the defensive presence or depth to compete against DeAndre Jordan, Blake Griffin, and the Clippers. And Chris Paul was still arguably the best point guard in the league. Steph still had to get some experience under his belt in order to reach his full potential. We took the Clippers to seven games, and played as well as we could. But we lost by 5 points on the road in game 7 of the first round.

After the season was over, we had exit meetings. I sat down with Coach Jackson and told him that I was thankful for all he had done and that I really felt we were on the precipice of something big. We got to talking about my off-season plans, and I told him about the treatment I was about to undergo. He was worried. "Don't play USA Basketball, Andre," he said. "You're doing too much. You've got to rest and get back healthy. This next season is going to be something entirely different. You watch."

I thanked him and went on my way. Hours later I found out from my Twitter feed that he was terminated by the team. That's how quickly things go in this business. I barely had time to process it because I was undergoing a medical procedure that had me feeling mostly out of it for the next week. It seemed as though I went under with one coach and came to with another. And that's the thing about professional sports. Everything is on a clock, and there is no time. There's no time to process, to sit with feelings, to take bigger stock of what's happening. There's no time to grieve or transition. Everything is always about who or what is next. Next man up. Coach Jackson had been a mentor and leader to us all season, and two days later it was time to put everything behind us and welcome the next man. I was about to be on my eighth coach in twelve years. So I knew the drill. Just try to be optimistic.

<hr>

If you put a gun to my head and offered me a million dollars, I still probably couldn't recall the details of my first meeting with Steve Kerr. He's just so cool, so plain-Jane. You could sit through an entire dinner where he was at the table and never notice him. But he's always paying attention, always noticing details. And he knows when to talk and when to listen. Steve and I connected on basketball immediately because we had both learned the game from Lute Olson. We saw the game the same way. He could see things about my game that I was feeling but hadn't quite found the words for. He recognized that I was still relying too heavily on the isolation, and that I could be an entirely different player in a ball-movement offense.

One of Steve's main qualities is that he's very even-keeled, very self-directed. He is who he is, he is happy with who he is, and he won't let anything, any pressure, any criticism, any bad looks, any unfair press, change him. When he came to us, we were already the number one team defensively in the league. Mark had made sure of that, and Steve wasn't the type of coach who would change everything up just to make it fit his image. He recognized where what we had was working, and he was perfectly happy to keep it that way. And he was not a screamer or a yeller. Just like the rest of the organization, he seemed to believe in us as players and as adults. He didn't have to yell at players to work hard, for example. He recognized that if a player wasn't working hard, that player *knew* he wasn't working hard. Everyone else knew he wasn't working hard. He would count on that to motivate that person. And if it didn't, then the player wouldn't see the floor and it was as simple as that.

When you look at the history of the game, his coaching style was, in a sense, the next evolution. In the first thirty years of the sport, coaches were the most powerful forces in the franchise. Because sports in the 1950s and '60s operated more like the military. Chain of command. John Wooden, the legendary UCLA coach, was maybe the most influential thinker in the philosophy of coaching. He focused on doing little things correctly and with honor and discipline. He stressed that the true job of an athlete was not to win but to rise to every occasion, give your best effort, and make those around you better as you did it. His message carried tremendous weight because his program had tremendous success. He won ten national championships with the UCLA Bruins, a feat no college coach has ever repeated and probably never will. And many of the NBA players who came through that program—Kareem Abdul-Jabbar, Gail Goodrich, Bill Walton, and Jamaal Wilkes—ended up in the Hall of Fame. His influence spread throughout the league through coaches and players who had either worked with him or tried to emulate his philosophy. During those years, there were very few max superstar players who could command a following on their own. That would have tilted the balance of power away from the coaches in a way that most people in the game thought was unhealthy. It was assumed that no matter how important a player was, no matter how talented, they were still going to treat the coach with deference.

Moving into the 1970s and '80s you began to see the emergence of the true superstar in the modern sense, players who were celebrity brands in their own right. But still, even the two biggest players of that era, Magic and Bird, were guys lauded for their team approach to the game. This was important for the league to push, because even as late as the mid-'80s games were still being played on tape delay. There simply were not enough people interested to show them live. The league was able to use Magic and Bird to make a narrative that they hoped would earn the trust of audiences that were curious about the sport but not yet committed. Their brand of basketball—humble attitude, well behaved, marketable, and smiling—became the brand that coaches around the league and even in colleges and high schools could point to and say, "See? This is how you win games!"

But by the '90s something else entirely was under way. A variety of economic and cultural forces had combined to make it possible for players to become more powerful, at least in the eyes of the paying public, than coaches. It began with Jordan, who was so good that not only did he become a brand, but—with the growing influence of rap pushing urban culture, with its love of sneakers, into the mainstream— his clothing and lifestyle brand became, in a sense, bigger than his basketball brand. In his wake, you had players like Allen Iverson, Tracy McGrady, Vince Carter, Shaq, and Kobe, whose sheer athleticism made them human highlight reels, and brought them absurdly priced shoe and marketing contracts that the league simply couldn't match. By the late '90s the power had swung back to the players, and a lot of coaches were more like featured extras in a production starring the player. Coaches of that era had to learn not just how to do X's and O's but how to manage celebrities on a team.

Steve represented the third phase of this. He had learned by playing on those Bulls teams with Michael Jordan and coached by Phil Jackson what it took to manage superstar talent. But having come up under Lute Olson and having also played with Gregg Popovich, he had a sense of the discipline, of the old-school. He was particularly gifted at managing both things simultaneously, and the end result was a straightforward and trustworthy approach.

"Andre, I just want you to come in and work every day, and have fun," he would say to me. "You guys love the game. I know you want to have fun, so go do it. I know you are a leader on this team, Steph's a leader. All I need to do is put you guys in the right position. Find our weaknesses, catch them. If we stay sharp, we can get a six-, seven-year run out of this thing." This was the type of confidence he had coming in. "You guys are great, I see what we have. We just gotta do a few things to take us over the top."

I came into camp that year still trying to heal my knee. It seems like every off-season I'm trying to heal a knee, and this one was no different. I wasn't as in shape as I wanted to be because I had spent the majority of the summer rehabbing, but I was willing to try to grind it out and find my way back into it. You never want to rush your recovery, but circumstances always conspire to force you to do just that. I had spent the summer taking it slowly, and I was excited to push through camp and see where we could get to in our second year together. I had a better feel for each of these guys now. I was aware that I was playing with some all-time great shooters and that I could trust the movement, because if I passed up a good shot, I knew the ball was probably going to come right back. But still, the opportunities for me as an offensive player were lessening. Steve was introducing concepts that were favoring the outside shot even more than we had before, and that simply meant that I was going to have to play with some balance and awareness. Rather than making the offense on my own, I could see that part of what was needed was for me to have a kind of meta-awareness of how everyone else's game was opening up. Knowing when to open the throttle, when to close it. I felt that as camp went on, I was finding a groove. I shot well, played well, ran the floor well. Steve came to me near the last day of camp.

"You've played well, Andre. You've earned the starting spot . . ."

I knew right then that there was only one reason he was telling me that. There was going to have to be a "but."

"But I think it's best for the team if you come off the bench. If we don't bring you off the bench, we're just not going to get as much from our second unit."

I had never, in my entire NBA career, come off the bench. A million things went through my head. Was he really saying I'd earned it, or was he just trying to soften the blow of telling me that I'd lost a step? Was this the beginning of the end for me? I didn't want to think so, but every player knows that his days are numbered, and when a starter is turned into a bench player, it's just one of those moments when you begin to wonder if the end is coming sooner than you think. It may sound as though it's all ego. I know it's easy for folks sitting at home to criticize a player for not wanting to come off the bench. But you have to understand the depth of it for NBA players.

From the time you are in your youngest years of the game, seven, eight, nine years old, you are told that you don't want to come off the bench. To do so makes you a scrub. As you grow, it becomes not only part of your identity but just the way you understand your job. It would be as if you were a journalist, had made a career as a journalist, and then after eleven years someone came to you and said, "We want you to keep writing articles, but we're going to put someone else's name on them." You would take exception and it would be a silly argument for someone to come to you and say, "All that matters is that the article is good in the end." That isn't all that matters. There is a certain way you are used to doing things, and it is a lot to totally upend it.

But I had to trust Steve. And I had to trust the organization. He and I saw the game the same way. If he said that the team would do better with me playing with the second unit, then I had to believe him. And most of all, I knew that whatever my personal feelings were about it, there was no conceivable way that starting a big ruckus over this was going to be anything other than terrible for the team.

Coming off the bench was entirely different from starting and it would take me all year to get used to it. When you start, you can kind of let the game come to you. Every game is different. Every player, every team, every contest has its own rhythm to it. As a starter, you can let that rhythm reveal itself to you in the first two minutes. You can take it in and figure out the plan. But coming off the bench feels like you're being thrown into an already moving wave. You're having to impose your will on whatever's happening. You've got to force things off the bench. That's not really my style. I didn't really know how to do that, and as the season started, the whole thing was even more confounding.

But Steve did have another vision for me. Every time he sent me in, he would say the same thing to me: "Andre, find the flow." And for some reason, I knew exactly what it meant. It meant get that ball moving, get it popping. Get motion and rhythm to our game, especially if we were down when it was time for substitutions. I had been thinking of it all wrong. My job wasn't to come in and create offense.

It was to come in and *find* where the offense lay. It was always there. I was to find it for our team, to uncover it and deliver it. And almost always it could be found through the movement of the ball.

People in my life, friends, family members, didn't understand. I would argue with my business manager Rudy all the time. He thought I was suffering from a lack of confidence. My close friend and basketball trainer Tyrell, who'd been working with me since I came into the league, said his friends were texting him things like, "You said Dre was nice. He fell off. He's over." And I could see where they were coming from. In my two previous roles, I had tried to just focus on doing my job, but the circumstances of the roster meant that I was still the face of the team, with my image on posters and programs. And this meant I would have ads and opportunities and clout. In this new role, however, I might spend twenty-four minutes on the floor and come away with 4 points and 3 assists.

It's one thing to agree with something and quite another thing to go out and live it game by game. I would have a good game, and know that I'd had a good game. I would feel focused and clean, showing up in the right spots, making the right plays, and we would win. But still, it would just feel weird that I'd had only one shot. It would get frustrating. To complicate matters, we were definitely winning. By the time we got to Christmas Day that year, we were 22-3. No one wants to be the guy who's complaining when everyone is winning. And we'd been having fun doing it. I would be on the sidelines cheering and jumping up and down with support for my team, but inside I was struggling. And it wasn't even about shooting all the time. There were some nights when I would feel like, "Man, just let me get the ball, draw a double-team, and pass."

Helping find the rhythm for my team worked. But finding my personal offensive rhythm within that never did. Sometimes I'd be open to shoot, but I would know that we'd had too many one-pass-and-shoot possessions in a row and that it was time to get the ball popping. So I would pass up the shot. After a while it was hard for me to attend to both my own rhythm and the team rhythm. They were frequently at odds. Sometimes I would come into the locker room at halftime and be pissed. I was literally out there on the floor killing my value. I could see it happening, possession by possession. What if this wasn't my last contract? What if I had come to Golden State only to descend into being a mediocre player? I knew those thoughts weren't going to help me, but it was human nature. This game takes a lot out of you. And the idea that you might not be getting everything you can out of it is troubling. It can make a person unravel. It always goes back to that question. How much would you take to give up a hip? When you give as much as you do to this game, when you know it may make it impossible for you to walk without pain again, you want to make sure you are getting everything you possibly can in return. Championships are good for you, but maximizing financial security may, in the long run, be even more important.

But even when I had my doubts, it was clear that there was absolutely no point in sabotaging the locker room with complaining. I could see what Steve was trying to accomplish, and the vision made perfect sense to me because he and I had learned the game the same way. We finished 67-15, one of the best records in franchise history, but I still ended the regular season feeling entirely out of sorts offensively. I had never gotten into my groove, and I was aware that offensively I was capable of so much more. Still there were moments toward the end of that season when I began to understand something greater about it. I would be working with the second unit, trying to see the game and transmit it to them as we ran. And I would start realizing that the more judicious I was about picking my offensive spots, the better everything went for me and for the team. I began to finally understand the meaning of the old cliché "Less is more."

I saw that in my playing, but I also saw that in my teammates'. By the time I'd gotten there, Stephen Curry was in the middle of a complete resurgence. Many people forget that his first few years in the league were marked by injury. People felt like he was never going to get it together well enough to play long-term. But he quietly underwent a complete transformation of how he used his body and played his game. It was an act of complete discipline and willpower, and freakish talent. It was the quintessential Steph Curry move.

There aren't that many people like him in this sport or anywhere else I've seen. Steph is truly as all-around a good guy as everyone makes him out to be. He comes from a very good family, as we've all seen on TV. His dad, Dell Curry, played in the league for many years and seems to have done a pretty tremendous job raising his son. There is not a mean bone in Steph's body. Of course he's insanely competitive, but he's also very genuine and very humble. But maybe the thing I noticed most about him after playing with him for a couple of years is that he is ridiculously athletically gifted. He excels at literally everything. Playing golf with him is boring because he hits the ball far and straight every single time. Then he can putt long and straight and put you out of the game by the first hole. It doesn't matter what the sport is, he dominates at it. You'll be playing darts and he'll hit triple twenties. We had a Ping-Pong tournament for the team as a way to break up the grind of a long season, and of course he ended up in the final match for that. Then another time the coaching staff took us to the baseball stadium, where we were allowed to play a game for fun. Steph was the pitcher, and of course he was firing strikes right down the line until it became time to hit, and then there he was, winning at that too. He hit two home runs that day in a major league stadium and he's not even a baseball player. Maybe Allen Iverson was the only other person I played with who was as all-around gifted as Steph Curry.

Overall my connection to those Golden State teams is as strong as to any team I've even been on. You often hear players say that they get along with all their teammates, but in this case it was really true. Each person was so unique, and the overall vibe was so good, that we just kind of got to enjoy being around each other. You had Klay Thompson, who really puts the "free" in free spirit. Laid-back doesn't even begin to describe him. He's just really about never causing any problems, always going along, always hanging out with the team. He's one of the easiest guys in the world to be around. His dad, Mychal Thompson, played for the Lakers alongside Magic, Kareem, and James Worthy, and you can tell that Klay came from that good home, that well-taken-care-of background. His dad is from the Bahamas, which is a very laid-back place, and you can see that trickle down to Klay. He like to chill, crack jokes, hang out with the fellas.

But like every professional athlete, he has another side to him. I watched from the sidelines the game in which he scored 37 points in a quarter against Sacramento. Even though it was a statistical anomaly and an all-time record, it was in a certain way exactly what you would expect from Klay. He is like Steph in the sense that he has the gene, the ability to become so caught up in a game that he's entirely unable to remember what happened twenty seconds ago. In a shooter this can be a tremendously helpful quality. Klay can go 0 for 7 from distance in the first two quarters of a game and literally have no idea that he's 0 for 7. His brain just doesn't track it. Steph is the same way. For these guys, there are no missed shots—all these guys see is the next one. That is a very unusual skill. Most players, myself included, simply aren't like that. If I miss three three-point shots in a row, I'm probably not shooting from distance for the rest of the game—that's just the way I am. I'm not trying to end a game 0 percent from three. But Klay is different. He simply does not care. He'll just keep shooting until it turns around. And it always turns around. That's how they can go from shooting 0 percent to ending the game hitting ten or twelve straight. It's just something, some incredibly focused, almost mercenary quality inside them.

A lot of times people will say that a player is "unconscious" when he or she is going off in a game. And from what I've seen with Klay, that's an accurate description. He gets a laser focus, and it seems like everything else disappears. Being the kind of player I am, that sometimes surprises me. My whole thing is to see the game, know the situation. As soon as I touch the ball, I'm immediately trained to look around me, know where everyone is, who's cutting where, how much time is on the clock, how many fouls each player has, how many we have collectively. That's probably why I would know that I was 0 for 3. But Klay, when he gets that laser focus, sees nothing but the hole. Sometimes he'll just launch a shot from ten feet beyond the arc early in a possession when we're down by like 2 points, and I'm yelling as soon as he gets the ball, "Klay! You're at half court, man!" It's like it truly never occurred to him. He just sees a shot he can make.

Once, we were doing a team-building exercise. The idea was to understand the connection between feelings of success and the way we sat in our bodies, versus how we held our bodies when we were talking about "failure." So everyone had to answer the question of what were their favorite moments in the game, what were the moments they felt the highest, and we were to notice what was happening in our bodies as we talked about it. When Klay's turn came, we all assumed he was going to say that his highest moment was the day he scored 37 points in a quarter against Sacramento. I mean, that was an NBA record! But he didn't. Instead he said, "My best moment was one night I caught a pass and I was like fifty feet from the basket and I was about to shoot it.

And all of a sudden, I hear Andre being like, 'What the fuck, Klay? You're fifty feet out.' And I thought about it for a second and shot it anyway. It went in, and I was like, 'Yeah, Andre, fuck you.'" We all had a good laugh at that. I was like, "Wow, really, dog? That was your best moment?" But that's just the way it is with him. He believes he is the best shooter in the world, like he's never going to miss. And he's not entirely wrong about that. I understand that attitude to an extent. He and Steph both went to small schools, they were both overlooked in a sense, and they have something to prove. And they have both turned out to be all-time great shooters. That's no coincidence.

As much as our team is animated by that love of the game, maybe the other biggest factor is that sense of being an underdog, of being overlooked and having to prove to the world that we belong here. We all have a little bit of that, but Draymond Green is the heart and soul of that idea on our team. All of us on the team came, of course, from different backgrounds—this is the case with all players. Some guys like Steph and Klay come from good homes, two parents, professional-athlete parents, and the game is with them from birth. You have other guys who come from basically nothing, but everyone around them recognizes that they can be the savior if they can just make it out of there. So everyone sacrifices for them, protects them, travels with them, sends them off to prep schools, spends all their money to make it work for them. But you have those kids like Draymond who were underdogs the entire time. Never the upper-middle-class kid with the basketball family, never the golden child or hood savior everyone rallied around to lift up. He had to put it all together on his own. That's why he has that bravado about himself. Because he wasn't supposed to be here at all.

And that alertness is maybe the most remarkable thing about him. I've heard fans criticize him for not having his head in the game, and I can't think of anything more ridiculous. He is a quite possibly the smartest, most focused basketball player I've ever seen. He's simply on another level. Almost a savant. He can remember plays from four years ago *in their entirety*, and he'll run you through the entire thirty-second sequence moment by moment. He'll remember his team's plays and he'll remember other teams' plays. He can call out their plays in the middle of games just based on the slightest indications. The position of the point guard and the way the center is cutting will tip him off, and he'll call it out to us. It's like he has an entire film library stored in his head and he can call it up to us at any time.

It can be said that he grew up in the hood, but with him you get the sense that the hood is what made him as attentive and focused as he is. He stays aware of his surroundings not only on the court but in the business of the game. He always knows the background on every player, what their salary is, when their contract or free agency is coming up. He pays attention to the college game, knows what players are coming out, where they're projected to go. He's one of those people who just enjoys everything about being in the NBA. There are some people who like this profession because of the fame and the money. I think Draymond enjoys his life in the league because he remembers where he's come from and how hard he's worked to maximize his potential, to gain the fruits of his labor. He's made a life for himself and the people around him and he's proud of that.

And we've seen people around the league get mad at him. He's become, nationally, something of an NBA bad guy, and as a team we understand why that is. We see the antics. Nobody's perfect, but it matters if they are good. If they care. If they work. Draymond's head is always in respecting the game of basketball, in knowing everything he needs to know and doing everything he needs to do in order to win. Does he stray off the path now and again? No doubt. But his intent is never to harm the team. It's to win. Plain and simple. People ask if we get frustrated, but for us it's like, "Man, that's our brother!" Of course, you get frustrated with your brother, temporarily. But the respect, the love for him you have, is permanent. We all get frustrated with each other the way all families get frustrated. We get on Klay for taking fifty-foot jumpers when we're up by three with ten seconds on the clock. We get on Steph for making lackadaisical passes. After we got Kevin Durant we would get frustrated with him for caring too much what people think. They get frustrated with me when I'm not aggressive or in attack mode. But at the end of the day, this is our family. And we will stay with it, no matter what.

Early in that first season, 2014–15, under Coach Kerr's offense, I started to know that we were potentially sitting on a championship team. The way the ball was moving, the way we were passing, the way Steph was shooting the ball—we were just wiping people out of the gym. And no one really saw it coming. Teams were still treating us like a small-market upstart. That was Steph's first MVP year. Draymond was starting, and he had brought a force to the defensive end. But it was the perfect force, because for all his energy, he was still always one of the smartest players on the floor at any given time. He could see the game unfolding two or three moves ahead, and he was an incredibly quick thinker. Also Bogut had really embraced Kerr and his philosophy. I always felt like Andrew was one of the best centers in the league, especially defensively, but once he broke his elbow, it kind of ate into his confidence. When he was clicking, he and Draymond were an unstoppable defensive force.

We got to the finals that year against Cleveland, and it seemed to happen faster than we could understand. We knew we were a good team, but I think all of us were surprised by the fact that we were somehow in the NBA Finals. It reminded me of the feeling in high school when I thought I might be good enough for my town, but I didn't know if I could hoop with those Chicago boys. Or when I was in college and was finding out that I might actually be good enough for the draft. It was the first time anyone on our entire team had been to the finals and none of us knew what to expect.

It's a spectacle. You think you've been under the microscope with sixty-seven wins, but it's nothing like the experience in a finals series. In our first practice, the media was let in about an hour or so after we started, as usual, and they get thirty minutes to watch us run. At that point, we're of course not doing anything serious. It's fluff—shooting drills, layup drills, that sort of thing. But I noticed as they began to file in, filling the seats and surrounding the court. Two minutes go by, five minutes go by, and I'm still seeing new people come in. I had never in my life attended a media event where it took five minutes for everyone to get in the room. There is an energy to it. You have to do NBA TV, ESPN, and local channels, and then you sit down in front of everyone for fifteen to twenty minutes. It's hard to explain to anyone else, but something shifts inside of you. You begin to feel the weight of the moment and the electricity of it. You become aware of just how big a deal this basketball game you're playing in is. It starts to feel like a world event. Reporters are there from Australia, China, Japan, Mexico, Brazil. It begins to seem odd that so many people the world over are watching what happens in a game that you're going to be playing in.

The night before the opening tip, I was just thinking about the game plan. I wanted to clear my mind but I couldn't. I found myself imagining scenario after scenario. It would stay that way throughout the entire series. It was not possible to turn it off between games. I could think of nothing but basketball. I was getting treatments seemingly around the clock. Icing, massages, putting a machine on my legs to stimulate blood growth. You go home at eleven o'clock or midnight after the game, and all you can think about is every play. You are living at home, but it's rough on your family, because you are essentially absent. I had to let my wife know that I appreciated how she puts up with me during the finals. Because as much as the regular season involves travel and commitments, the finals take over all aspects of your life in a much more complete way. There is no you left.

We split the first two games, and both of them went to overtime. We lost the third and found ourselves in a 2–1 hole. After game 3, I ran into a VC, close friend, and company starter I knew named Clarke Miyasaki. I will remember this conversation as long as I live. "Clarke," I said, "I figured it out. We're gonna win this thing. Watch." He thought I was crazy. On paper Cleveland had the advantage. But internally I had seen what was happening on that floor. Steph was picking apart their defensive scheme, and Klay was finding some open shots as a result. Which meant they were going to start doubling someone soon. I could see that I was about to get a lot more offensive opportunities, and I didn't want to say it too soon, but my body was feeling, somehow, right for the first time all year. My shot was feeling good and easy, and I started to wonder if I was going to be able to have my own flow while I kept the team flow.

Coach had recognized that late in game 4, when he went with a smaller lineup—Draymond at center, Steph and Klay in the backcourt, and me and Harrison Barnes rounding out the front line—which Cleveland had a very hard time defending. We could run pick-and-rolls out of that group, and they had to double Steph, which meant that

I could shoot or make a play. Defensively we could switch up whenever we wanted, because their bigs weren't really an offensive threat.

And it meant that I was going to be guarding LeBron.

Much has been made about that. I read an article where someone suggested that me guarding LeBron was the difference in the series. I don't know if that's true, but I do know that there is no such thing as shutting down LeBron James. He's going to get his points, and he's got the ball in his hand so much, and he's such a smart player that he's going to make the most out of every chance he gets. But I knew that if I played him just as smartly as he played the game, then we wouldn't have to send two people, which would stifle their offense.

You have to be smart to defend LeBron James, or at least I had to. You have to understand his game and how he thinks and think along-side him but also ahead of him. I remembered my rookie year back in Philly, when I was given a tape with every guard in the East's best moves, and how I learned those moves, studied them so I could think alongside them and therefore ahead of them. I had to do that in rapid time with LeBron. The key was to be quick, and I had to be ready to take the first hit. I saw that his first offensive move almost always in-volves some contact with you to get you out of the way. And because he is so strong, it usually works. But I realized that if I could with-stand that hit without moving, then he would have to change his plan in mid-step. Next was to always know where the ball was going to be. So whichever way he went, I just got good at guessing where the ball was going to end up. I had to anticipate. If I missed, I missed. But if I stayed focused, I could get a strip about six out of ten times. But I was comfortable doing that because I knew that I had Draymond behind me, who was just as good as I was at anticipating LeBron's moves. Then you had to know which way to send him based on what his rhythm was for that particular game. If you watched him for the first five minutes of a game, you could tell what was working for him that night and what wasn't. If his jumper was falling, then you knew you had to be right up on him. If he was going to be forcing the issue and driving to the basket, then you wanted to set off him a bit, dare him to shoot. You were trying to get into his mind, make him second-guess himself. In that sense it was like high-speed chess. You were guessing what his move was going to be and you knew he was basing his moves on what he thought you expected.

Once we went small and opened up the game offensively and shut it down defensively, we knew we had them locked. I had gotten my rhythm back at exactly the right time, and with about two minutes left in game 6, the reality started to dawn on me. We weren't sure, we didn't want to believe it, but we wanted to believe it. We were up by about 10 points, but still we knew it could slip away. We were terrified that some fluke thing would happen. Then they cut it to 7. Then to 6. We were up by about 7 with a minute to go. That had to be it. We couldn't lose it now, could we?

LeBron came over and started dapping everyone up. Good game, good series, congratulations. But still we needed the clock to wind down, and it just *wasn't winding down fast enough.* Meanwhile J.R. Smith hit a ridiculous three with about thirty-three seconds left to bring the game to back within one possession, and none of us could believe it. It's the most unnatural state you can think of. Are you about to celebrate the most important moment in your sports career? Or is it just another day at the office? We really couldn't tell. We had no idea what to believe. I missed a free throw with about ten seconds left, but it was still a two-possession game. Out of the time-out, J.R. launched a thirty-footer that missed. Steph grabbed the rebound and there was just this moment where I was looking around for someone else to confirm what I thought was happening. It seemed like we had just won the NBA championship, but it was almost like I couldn't be sure until I made eye contact with someone else. The clock wound down. Two seconds . . . one second. Steph threw the ball in the air. Confetti came down from the ceiling, and I could not believe anything that was happening. I grabbed the ball and made sure I would never let go of it.

In an instant, the floor was crowded with NBA officials, celebrities, players from other teams. It was madness. I just remember Justin Holiday was hugging me. Everything was happening so fast. I was overcome thinking about everything I had gone through to suddenly get to this moment. This one right here. I was just screaming and yelling and hugging anyone I saw. I saw Kiki VanDeWeghe from the league office—a guy no one ever likes to see because he's the one who delivers the fines—and for some reason I was hugging Kiki. I just didn't care. All my friends were there, and it was a madhouse. Soon my wife brought my son up and I could see in his eyes how incredibly happy he was for us. That was the best part. He was lit up all over.

Meanwhile they were setting up the stage for the presentation of the trophies, and everyone's family was appearing. Draymond's mom, Steph's wife, Klay's dad. Everyone is hugging and congratulating each other and there's just this feeling that something really special was happening. I remember taking a moment to look at everything. Confetti in the air, music playing, everyone hugging and crying, sweat not even dried on your uniform. It was hard to believe that only minutes ago we were playing a game and now we were suddenly champions of the world. We were blessed. That's all I kept thinking about. We were blessed in this moment. Seventy to 80 percent of players never even make it to the NBA Finals. Why us? How us? We hadn't expected it. It was the most amazing thing. We had just put our heads down and played basketball. And when we looked up again, the air was filled with confetti.

———

M aybe the parade should have been the first sign.

We arrived early at the practice arena, around 8:00 a.m., with our families and friends, kids and childhood homies, and we were still celebrating. I had been in LA on some late-night talk show—I don't even remember which. It had been a nonstop party. Assembling for the parade, we were still high-fiving and hugging. More speeches were made. Taking pictures with the family and friends of everyone in ownership. Signing hats and water bottles for people you've never seen around the facility before. Nike had sent over all the fresh new championship gear that we were excitedly putting on. Food was eaten from a luxurious spread. And then we were to mount our individual buses to go down the streets of Oakland like conquering heroes.

But it took us half an hour just to get to the parade route—thirty minutes of sitting in the sun on the back of a bus on a random side street downtown. By 10:00 a.m. we were already exhausted. And we hadn't even started. The day wore on. And on and on. The fans gave us energy, and that was the best part. Running side to side, high-fiving kids—there's no joy like it. It was truly the most beautiful thing. But then once we pulled up to the grandstand, it would be another hour before all the buses arrived. At one point we were just napping. With a million people downtown, waiting for the rally to start, we were just sleeping. The parade was amazing at first and then exhausting. Maybe it should have been the first sign. Winning the championship was amazing. Being the champion could be debilitating.

Year two with a coach is always a better year than year one. At least if the coach is not terrible, and Steve Kerr is not. He has a brilliant offensive mind and he is really good at teaching the game in all its forms. We had run through the first year, but now the offense would have extra layers. We were comfortable with each other, and people were coming into their primes. The 2015–16 season felt like going 90 miles per hour on cruise control. We're coming at you, we're running you over, it's not going to be hard. We were taking joy in the game, and in the early part of the season the fame had not yet become a problem.

We began on a twenty-four-game winning streak, which was amazing at first, but in retrospect I can see the seeds of our undoing in that first run. The media began to over-cover us. Our press conferences were going from five reporters to forty-five reporters. People were asking repetitive questions, about clothes and entertainment. Steph and Klay would end up on blog posts for just walking down the street. We had expected that to some extent, but Hollywood reporters were covering even the last guys off the bench as though they were celebrities. With that many reporters the questions get both stupid and repetitive because everyone is looking for a story. I did about five stories in a row on my sleep habits, because someone had heard that I was starting to get into sleep hygiene. After a major hit, media would just try to duplicate the story.

On top of that, you start to become something of a traveling road show for the NBA. We got our schedule and it involved insane stretches on the road, crisscrossing time zones like we had never done before. Our streak ended on the last night of a seven-game road trip where we had gone from Utah to Charlotte to Toronto to

Brooklyn, back to Indiana, back to Boston, and then to Milwaukee. That kind of trip would have been unthinkable for us even two years ago. Just as players have a short window to get everything they can, I started realizing that the NBA had a short window to get everything it could out of our Little Engine That Could feel-good story. Ticket prices were shooting up everywhere we played. I used to be able to get my homeboys tickets to games in Milwaukee for like $100 a pop. Good seats too. Now they were talking about $300 for mediocre seats. Friends who had been so happy before were now complaining about where they were sitting. Everywhere we went, arenas were sold out, and teams were playing us like it was an elimination game. When Milwaukee finally edged us out in our twenty-fifth game, they had confetti coming from the ceiling like they had just won a gold medal. All this and the season was only one-quarter of the way over.

We were starting to hear talk about the Chicago Bulls and their seventy-two-win season. It was an impossible record to break. And it had stood for twenty years. Coach Kerr had played on that team, and he hated all the talk about us breaking that record. He knew how much that took away from the task at hand. But the thing gained a momentum of its own and soon it was bigger than him. Luke Walton was serving as interim coach, because Steve was out with back issues, and you could see that Luke was torn on what to do. He knew that the record would be valuable. And as the story grew, so, too, did Luke's sense that he didn't want to be the one to mess it up. Furthermore, there was a sense not only among the league at large but among ourselves that we were approaching invincibility. Slowly but surely the rotations began to reflect that we were trying to keep that streak going, rather than preparing for the postseason run.

We started to lose track of our bigger goal of perfecting our game, of peaking at the right time. We just needed to win that night, and the next, and the next. There were games when we didn't play our best and you could tell early that it was an off night. But instead of just taking the loss and regrouping and adjusting, the starters were staying in, playing forty, forty-one, forty-two minutes a night. We started feeding our own egos, even though we were just barely getting by a couple of games. We often took the floor that year with the expectation that we could smack anybody. It's not that we shouldn't have had that confidence, because that's what all teams need. But we were playing with a switch: the idea that we could turn it on or off whenever we felt like it. What was missing was appropriate fear, appropriate respect for the fact that we could be beaten in any given game.

And we chased. We chased that record with everything we had because we needed to be not only the best team in the league, but the best team of all time. Everywhere we went, Michael Jordan and the Bulls loomed over us. They had done something once that no team had done before or since in the history of the game. And it made sense that we were excited by the idea that we could match that. I would look around the practice facility and get goose bumps thinking about the fact that this assembly of dudes—Klay, with his easygoing nature and absurdly quick release; Steph, with his incredible earnestness and genuine humility; Draymond, who would bark at anyone, anytime—might have just stumbled themselves onto a team that would go down in basketball history. The allure was too much to resist.

But the flip side was that in every arena, guys were having the best games of their lives against us. Players who didn't normally make shots were making them. It was basketball, basketball, basketball. In the pressers, in interviews, every night you were getting booed mercilessly, and every young player on the planet was trying to make his name at your expense. There was just a mental fatigue that set in. I noticed the younger guys struggling with it more, but we were all feeling it. It got to a point where you just needed a break from the Warriors sideshow, but people kept showing up for it. There was no end in sight. By the time we got our seventy-third win, it was the last game of the regular season, and I couldn't believe that the important basketball was just beginning.

We ran through Houston in five games and had about the same amount of trouble with Portland. Then came Oklahoma City. People always ask me what the hardest team I've ever faced in my life was, and it was that Oklahoma City Thunder team with Kevin Durant and Russell Westbrook in the Western Conference finals. I had never seen anyone play like that. Durant was on fire that series. It was the best defense he could muster and it was stifling. And they had a huge lineup with Steven Adams and Serge Ibaka up front. Even their power forward was six foot ten, and all these guys could switch as well as we could. Serge Ibaka was versatile, and Westbrook was just a machine, attacking you relentlessly every single possession. It was like he had a battery pack with extra energy in it. Meanwhile, KD was scoring 50 points every night. We knew that we had to play "A" basketball. "A minus" ball would get us eliminated. And it almost did. We went down three games to one, and it was looking very shaky. I was so focused, the pressure was so great, that in our home no one was having fun. But deep down I felt like if any team could come back from being down 3–1, it would be us.

In our shoot-around meeting before game 5, Steve told us what we needed to hear. "I know we're going to get this game tonight at home," he said. "But that next game, game six in Oklahoma City, an elimination game, is going to be the hardest game we've ever played. Period. It will never get harder than that. But I can tell you something else. It's going to be given to us. I just know it. We're going to get this game. It will be given to us."

I don't know what he meant by that or how he understood it. But those words echoed in my head all week. And he was right. Game 6 in Oklahoma City is still the hardest game we've ever played. But somehow he knew and we knew that it was not going to be over. Klay tends to play big in elimination game 6s, and this was no exception. With 41 points, 11 of 18 from three, he was the reason we won that game. When we came back home for game 7, we just knew. I don't know how, but we just knew.

We were matched with Cleveland in the finals for the second time in a row. And they wanted revenge. It was three days later when we tipped off for game 1 and we quickly jumped out to a 2–1 lead. They were better this year, but so were we. And Coach Kerr was doing a great job of recognizing where we had advantages and playing them up. Fatigue was setting in for all of us. That Oklahoma series had taken a great deal out of us. But we knew that we could still rally if we could just keep it together. Then game 4 happened.

I've watched the play a thousand times. I saw it happen on the floor, and I've seen it happen in replay after replay. LeBron and Draymond got tangled up on a screen, and LeBron tossed Draymond to the hardwood. The play was still happening, so both players tried to get back into it, Draymond by getting up off his back, and LeBron by stepping over Draymond, who was still on the floor. Draymond got offended that LeBron was stepping over him and flailed his arm, hitting LeBron in the crotch. None of this was called, by the way. The referees let all this slide. Then, moments later, when Dray and Bron got into it over a rebound, a whistle was blown. The two of them jawed back and forth and were assessed with double technicals.

That night after the game was over, the league office reviewed the footage and determined that Draymond's swinging his hand was a flagrant foul, and since it was his fourth in the postseason, he would have to miss game 6.

Everything is a story. Everything is blown out of proportion. Everything is capitalized for financial gain. This is simply the way the league works. Sometimes you can tell that a decision is going to be made not because of the rules, but because of the story. All season long, Draymond had been the story. Part of it was because of the way he was. But it was also because of the way he was on our team. Most of what he did I saw happening on every floor in every arena around the country from every bench player with an edge. But a story had been created that Draymond Green was out of control and each event served to push that narrative. So by the time that game had ended, you could spend fifteen seconds on Twitter and tell that the league was going to suspend him. Because the decision was never made in response to the event. Basketball is entertainment. It's live, improvisational storytelling. So decisions will always be made in response to the story. There are going to be those who disagree, but I've been around the game a long time. And it's as plain to me as anything is.

What else can I say about that series. We watched it slip away, but in a sense it felt as though we never had a grasp on it to begin with. We were playing against something much larger than the Cleveland Cavaliers, even though, to their credit, they played in rare form. We were playing against a growing tide of our own celebrity that we didn't collectively know how to understand or manage within the game. We were playing against emotional and physical fatigue and an eight-month circus for which we were anything but prepared.

So by the time LeBron chased me down in the final seconds of game 7 and delivered one of the most awesome defensive plays I've ever seen, I already knew that it was over. Kyrie Irving hitting that big three to go up 92–89 a minute later only sealed the deal. We had already made irreversible mistakes. Momentum shifts, tides change. Centers get injured, backs spasm. And games get lost and they never come back again.

I barely have a memory of walking out of the arena that night. I saw Dave Chappelle, who has always been one of my heroes. I said, "What's up?" But our conversation was short. We didn't deserve to win. That's what I was thinking. We didn't deserve to win and I just wanted to go home. I wanted to be around my good friends. My wife, my son. Mustafa Shakur, who I had played with in college. My trainer Tyrell. People who knew me from before. I just wanted to be around people I trusted. I just wanted some love and a pizza and to sleep for three days straight.

08

The Seventy-Fourth Win

There would be no talk of a record next season, no talk of seventy-three wins. It had killed us. Plain and simple. You could point to and debate all the bizarre things that happened in that series: the fouls, the ejections, the suspensions, the Block. And you could debate how differently the season might have gone had any of those things not happened. But the only thing that was completely clear to me and to all of us was that every decision we had made in order to get to seventy-three wins had cost us the title. Was it worth it?

It would depend on what happened next. If that were to turn out to be our very last shot at the title, I can guarantee that every man on that 2015–16 Warriors team would have spent the rest of their lives thinking about how we had a title and we slowly, painfully, and surely let it slip away. And that all we had gotten out of it was seventy-three wins, a record that would forever have an asterisk. "Yeah, but they didn't win the title." This season would not just be about redemption. It would be about all of our futures.

I had been hearing rumors about our team acquiring Kevin Durant since around the midpoint of the prior season. It's not uncommon for a player to know a lot more about these pending deals than the press does. Most of us know better than to share what we hear from the staff with members of the media, but the conversations were definitely happening. Often on the Warriors squad, we would find out about deals in the works because an assistant would come to us and ask what we thought. "We're looking at such and such a player. Do you think he'd fit here? What have you heard about him?" The NBA is like a large company where everyone is a coworker, so the guys on other teams are not just opponents, they're colleagues. You've played with them in summer leagues or against them in conference tournaments in college. You used to crack jokes with them in the cafeteria at basketball camp when you were fifteen. You've been together at weddings and parties, off-season barbecues and golf tournaments. And if you don't exactly know them, you know enough people who know them to make it so that you have a real sense of who they are both on and off the court. But even if you just know a guy because you've played his team six or more times over the course of a season, you also observe dynamics, behavior, habits, and attitudes up close. So players have a very good sense of how a guy will fit in on a new team, and if the front office or an assistant GM is smart, they will pull up beside you casually in the training room and float a potential trade by you for your thoughts. It hadn't reached quite that level yet with Kevin, but we were definitely hearing whispers around the organization that they were going to try to make something happen.

So Kevin Durant to the Warriors was not a far-fetched idea for any of us when the 2016 season was over, and we knew what that would mean. We would run the league. Period. He was the best pure scorer in the game. An excellent shooter with ball handling, and an all-time great finisher at the rim. He was an offensive juggernaut. And as a seven-footer (yes, I know he's listed as six-nine, but c'mon) with a seven-four wingspan, he was incredibly hard to defend. We got to see that when he pushed us to seven games about a month before, and it took basically everything we had to get out of that Western Conference final with a win.

There are only two weeks between the end of the season and free agency, and that year I was basically just trying to get over what had happened in the finals. I was not surprised by the outcome, but I was surprised by how much it hurt. It hurt emotionally, of course, but it hurt physically too. I was tired and aching. My knee and hips were killing me, and I couldn't seem to get enough sleep, no matter what I did. Those first two weeks were a blur, almost like a hangover. I did my best to show up for my family, for golf, for business meetings. But mostly I felt like I was living through Jell-O. I needed something else to happen.

That something came with a text from the front office days after the end of the season. "You guys want Kevin Durant?" It was just that simple. Who wouldn't? We were told that he was hosting teams in the Hamptons on July 30 and that it could be good if we went. This was where the amount of respect that the organization had shown to us paid off. There would be a lot of players who would balk at the idea of going to do something like that. "Why are you trying to get me to do your job?" they might say. And that's an understandable viewpoint when you are playing for a team that has largely treated you as a commodity or a workhorse for the entirety of your time with them. It felt just like it did in college: you're only interested in me not because of who I am as a person but because you need something from me now. But this organization felt different. Because Steph was our superstar, and his attitude was always team-first, we all embraced that attitude and the front office reflected it. So when it was time for us to ride for our team, it was no question. We had all played with KD on the USA Basketball national team, so we knew that our best shot was to assemble a squad to go out and convince. Me, Klay Thompson, Steph Curry, and Draymond Green.

We thought of it as a fun trip too. We'd had a grind of a season and it would be nice to kick it with these guys absent the intense pressure of a championship run and chasing an NBA record. We would get to hang out a bit, have a decent dinner. Our whole attitude for that trip was relaxed and at ease, especially with Klay along. This was a guy who knew how to chill. Overall, we just used the trip to enjoy the moment and each other's company. This was the attitude we had when we walked into the house Kevin had rented. The air was mild, and you could smell the sea salt in the Atlantic breeze, the sound of the waves gently floating on the summer air. I took a moment to take it all in. It was a moment. Here were five wealthy black men, living in circumstances light-years beyond the wildest dreams of our parents, of our ancestors.

We met with Kevin for about an hour and a half, and like many good meetings, it was more conversation than pitch. We knew that we had what he wanted, so the plan was just to be honest about what we had. I had an instinct that the word of the day should be simplicity. Honesty. No crazy sizzle reels of him dunking on us or any of that high-tech nonsense. Just keep it real. We told him that we would have fun playing some basketball. That was it. No one on this team had an ego, no one cared who shot the ball and who didn't. We answered his questions about what the Bay Area was like, the good and the bad. We knew that one thing about Kevin was that when it came to basketball, he didn't just like to play. He loved to hoop. He loved the game in its purest form, and we felt that this team, the way we had it set up, with the offensive philosophy and the personalities we had on board, was a place where he could come to hoop.

But I knew the media would kill him if he made this decision. And I knew that if I were in his position, that's what I'd be worried about. I had a flashback to my days in Philadelphia. I knew what it was like to be hated, to spend every day trying to prove someone else wrong. Steph and Klay had always been loved. And Draymond was only beginning to embrace his NBA-heel thing. "Look," I said, "we can all do our best to take the heat off of you. But the most important thing is that *you* have to not give a fuck. Who cares what they say about you? They're either going to love you or hate you. It's always gonna be one or the other, no matter what you do. I mean, if you stay where you're at and you're not happy, what good is it? So what's more important? For you to enjoy your life being where you want to be, but with a bunch of strangers not liking your decision? Or to be where you're not enjoying your life, but with a bunch of strangers approving of you?"

We were sitting outside in this kind of garden area. There had been a much more official meeting inside during the previous hour with Kerr, Joe Lacob, Bob Myers, and Kevin's agent, Rich Kleiman—all the suits. Steve had compiled a bunch of clips to show Kevin where he'd fit from an X's and O's perspective. Bob Myers had gotten some kind of virtual-reality presentation together that was supposed to not only highlight Kevin's role as a Warrior but create a sense of the tech advances of the Bay Area. All of it was cool, but as the day wore on, there was an increasing sense for all of us, front office included, that this was just background noise to him. At a certain point, just the five of us— me, Steph, Klay, Draymond, and Kevin—had stepped outside to talk among ourselves. Kevin had been around this business his whole life and was wise to the game. He knew that every team was going to be coming in with a script and a bunch of canned lines about how they were going to welcome him to the family and he'd finally be home. We'd all been recruited before. What he really wanted, what he really needed, was the real deal from the players. And most importantly, he needed to hear it from Steph, because he knew that Steph had (potentially) the most to lose by him coming. He not only had to see that Steph would say it was all good, but he also had to see that Steph meant it. And that was good news for us, because if there's one thing I've learned about Stephen Curry, it's that he means what he says.

The five of us were outside alone and it was midmorning. The humidity was just getting started, despite the cooling breeze coming in from the Atlantic. There wasn't much more to say. We had all made our pitches. And I had tried to give him the veteran's perspective I had at this point in my career. But still, we were one of five teams he was receiving that week. Kevin thanked us for coming out, hugs and pounds were exchanged, and we were on our way, all of us piling back in the minibus we had arrived in together because we thought it would give the appearance that we were truly a band of brothers. No one spoke until the van was on the road. The mood in the car was humble, not celebratory. We didn't feel like we had nailed anything. We had just been ourselves. If it worked out, that would be great. If it didn't, then that would mean it wasn't supposed to. But deep down I had some doubts. I remembered the searching look on Kevin's face as he imagined what he'd have to confront with the media and fans.

Two days later, Kevin Durant was a Golden State Warrior. I was probably the most surprised of all of us.

―――

As the off-season wore on, I had to do more than work out and stay in shape. I needed to take serious medical interventions in order to get ready for another year on the hardwood. I was getting MRIs on my knees and hips, and undergoing a procedure called PRP injections, which in essence is when they take blood out of your body and spin it a trillion times in order to increase the white blood cells that promote healing and recovery. I had learned about the procedure from Kobe Bryant, who made use of it in order to play well into his later years. As a player who had come to the NBA at eighteen, was the star on his team, and had won five championships, Kobe had logged more minutes than pretty much anyone else in the league. So whatever he was doing to keep dragging himself out there year after excruciating year was something I needed to do. I was thirty-two years old at this point, and my body was feeling it. Even with tremendous discipline and incredibly focused eating and exercise habits, there's only so much you can will yourself to do. This blood-spinning thing was bizarre and a little bit ghoulish, but it was necessary.

The whole process takes seven days. First you sit there for five minutes giving blood. Sometimes I would get lightheaded, other times not. And then they place the blood in a centrifuge, spinning it around at phenomenal rates of speed while you sit there, looking up at the ceiling and thinking about how it is that your life has led you to a German clinic, where someone in a lab coat is stealing your blood seemingly by the gallon. Then they start injecting the newly white-celled blood in the various sites of your injuries, in my case hips and knees, and then you go on your way. Each visit takes about thirty minutes, and you do it for seven days while your body distributes the new extra-strength blood. You have to exercise every day that week to maximize blood flow, but you can't do anything too strenuous. So it's stretches, Pilates, yoga, biking, and light lifting—but no running. After seven days of it, you're back to full strength. And in my case, I started pushing it at the gym as soon as I could. You can begin to feel slight differences right away, after about two or three days, but it's about two or three months before it really takes hold. It's literally like having a new body. If only it would last.

Preseason prep after two deep postseason runs is very up and down. Some days you hit the gym and you feel like you could do this every day for the rest of your life. The shot is going, the weights are smooth, your body feels like it's working. Other days it's as though you have bricks tied to your ankles and the idea of going onto a court with ten other guys banging around for forty-eight minutes over eighty-two games plus the postseason seems like an absolute joke. You don't even know if you can stand twenty minutes on a practice court by yourself. But the thing is, you do. You just work through it because you know that no matter how bad it feels to go, it will feel much worse to quit. For the last two weeks of the off-season, I was doing two-a-days. Weights and training in the morning, then coming back at night and shooting. And shooting. And shooting and shooting. I like to shoot until I literally can't shoot anymore. It's the closest thing I'll ever come to feeling the way some people describe drugs. I start to lose all sense of my body, of even having a body. I just go until there is nothing left, past fatigue, past boredom, past annoyance. I go past thoughts about the last season, about the world.

Soon there is literally nothing left except the ball and the net and my breath.

***

We knew going into the 2016–17 season that if the Warriors were a sideshow before, with Kevin aboard it was going to be full-blown traveling circus. Ticket prices would explode everywhere we went. Every shoot-around in every town would see dozens more reporters than those for other teams. But oddly, I didn't feel pressure going into the season. Collectively we did not have a sense of "championship or bust." It was something beyond that. We knew that winning was what we were supposed to do, and so if we did our work, we would win. If we did not, we would lose. It was that simple. Losing the year before had hurt, but it didn't linger, at least for me. I wanted to win this year, but I knew that if we did not do our work, then we did not deserve it. And that was all there was to it.

The season began with San Antonio at home. This was supposed to be a marquee matchup for the NBA, as the Spurs had Kawhi Leonard, a guy who was kind of a quiet superstar. Quiet in the sense that you didn't hear or see a whole lot about him online—he had no "brand" to speak of—but superstar in the sense that he could flat-out ball and the media was beginning to take notice. He had developed something of a quiet-assassin story around him, and he was known for locking folks up defensively. On the surface, a perfect fit for his team: quiet, fundamental, and deadly. San Antonio was still considered a dynasty of sorts, even though there was starting to be a sense that the window might be closing on their dominance. It was their first year of the post–Tim Duncan era, but they still had Manu

Ginobili and Tony Parker, and Gregg Popovich was still the greatest coach in the league. It was good for the press and the league to think of every team as beatable, so opening up against a highly respected San Antonio team made for a great story. If they handled us as we came off a loss in the finals, it would be a great way to show that the West was truly up for grabs.

That was a tough game, and we were basically thrashed by a San Antonio roster that was much more cohesive and gelled than we were. We lost by nearly 30 points and trailed the whole game, save for a few minutes in the first quarter. For the press it was the ultimate sign that we had been pretenders to the throne and couldn't hang with the real elite teams of the Western Conference, especially as Cleveland was the other opening-day team and they had beat the Knicks by nearly 40 points. But for us, we were exactly where we were supposed to be. You cannot expect to add a new piece to the existing roster and suddenly have everything flowing. It would take some time for us to understand how it would all work together, and we would learn during the season. Our attitude was basically like, "Tough break. Who's next?"

We won the next four but got blown out by a young Lakers team, and then went on to win twelve straight. And this was as we were still getting to know how this thing was going to work. It was starting to become clear to me that we had the capacity to put something nearly unbeatable on the floor. Not that we were necessarily there, but that we *could* be if we were able to get all the parts working together smoothly.

We swung back through LA on December 7 to face the Clippers, another team the press had tried to make into a West Coast rival. They were talented, but we had beaten them seven times in a row. Nonetheless, it was a nationally televised game, and those are always unpredictable. The phenomenon of teams getting up for our visit like it was game 7 of the finals was even more pronounced when the game was on national television. We were a little sloppy offensively—ten turnovers, which would be unacceptable for some teams, but we were coming to realize it was part of the game with us. We did best when we moved the ball around a lot (we had 32 assists that game), and when we moved the ball around, we turned it over. That was just how it was. If we could keep that number under fifteen or so, then we felt we'd be alright. Mostly I remember that game because that was around the time it started to feel like I had my legs back. We beat them 115–98, and I had twenty-five minutes off the bench. The PRP injections back in September were definitely taking effect, and I felt like I might just make it through this alive after all.

We followed that up with a late-night trip to Utah to face the Jazz the next day. Salt Lake City has always had a certain effect on me as a player. I always feel—I don't know how else to say it—*blacker* when I'm in Utah. Something very uncomfortable is triggered in me when I play in front of that crowd. Not necessarily because they were any worse than any other crowd (though they were passionate). It had more to do with the kinds of thoughts that go through a black man's head when he's on a basketball court. You try not to let the discomfort creep into your game, but I defy anyone to be a black person on a floor in shorts and a tank top being screamed at simultaneously by eighteen thousand white people, who are flipping you off and spitting and foaming at the mouth, and not feel some deep, primordial, almost-cellular sense of threat. It's just not possible. It would never be possible, but everything felt much more ominous because this was two weeks after Trump had been elected.

I was not surprised by how incredibly and virulently racist this country is. I grew up in Springfield, after all. But what did worry me was that I began to wonder how much of my safety was based on the fact that even though people were racist, racism was still socially unacceptable. People were racist, but no one wanted to be *called* racist. They weren't trying to be out in public about it, which meant that I felt safer in public. But what we had seen over the past year had changed that. There were Nazi rallies and swastikas and people marching in the streets under the Confederate flag. There were murders of black people in churches and on the street, attacks against Muslims. This is the kind of stuff that runs through your head when you are in an arena surrounded by white people who have paid money to express how much they hate you. On the one hand, it's just a game. But on a much deeper level, it can never be.

We were up at halftime in that game—big. And then all of a sudden it was close again. It was a phenomenon we were noticing more and more. Games tightening up even though we were clearly outplaying the opponent, especially on the road. We would be clearly smacking a team around, and then they would start getting foul calls that would change the momentum of the game. I've been around this sport for decades, and it's not unclear to me what is happening, but it's one of those things that you're not allowed to say anything about, lest you get fined. So you try not to say too much or take it too seriously. You try not to be paranoid. But that night I heard a referee say to a teammate, "Don't look at me." There was something about that phrase. It stuck with me, echoed in my mind. But I was trying to stay in a good place mentally. I was trying to just play better and find the best iteration of my role with the team. I was just trying to keep it positive. I knew what could happen to me if I didn't. Those dark days in Philadelphia were not far enough behind me.

That road trip went on forever, it seemed. Three different time zones, Los Angeles, Utah, Memphis, Minnesota, New Orleans. It was taking its toll and we were struggling mentally. We were adjusting not only to playing together, but also to collectively facing the heightened pressure of each team circling our night on their calendar. The hardest games are the home games right before a road trip and right after, and our next game was at home against New York, another nationally televised affair. It was here that I was noticing that we were playing down to our competition. Carmelo Anthony and Derrick Rose were both out, and Kristaps Porzingis was a good player, but he struggled that night, shooting only 30 percent from the field. Offensively, we racked up something like 40 assists, and there was some stellar passing. I hit Kevin on the elbow with a sweet behind-the-back pass, and he in turn found Ian Clark, who drained a twenty-four-footer. It was a good moment, because I could see that Kevin was picking up on what we were doing. He was finding passes in motion, keeping defenders off balance, and that bode well for us. But defensively we struggled. We won handily, but I went into the locker room that night feeling like we had sold ourselves short.

That Christmas, the NBA, as it always did, set up a rematch of the finals. It was our first time seeing Cleveland since they had beaten us in the final minutes of game 7, and we were trying not to take it too seriously, but the press around the event was absurd. Another nationally televised game meant longer TV time-outs, more press people and suits around the court and the hallways, more celebrities showing up and trying to get back to the locker room. It was pretty silly. Not to mention that Christmas Day games are just hard because you're away from your family. You feel kind of resentful of the whole charade, like the league is trying to create drama that isn't really there. We didn't want to play into the story that this was a "rematch." We tried instead to treat it as a regular season game, just one more experience along the road of getting ourselves in shape for a postseason run. But nonetheless the drama was hard to avoid. Reporters were asking us stupid questions about the beef between Draymond and LeBron, trying to set up a rivalry between Steph and Kyrie Irving. As the game progressed, we could see that we simply did not have control. It was close for three and a half quarters, and we led most of the way, but down the stretch we let it slip through our fingers in a way that was uncomfortably close to how game 7 had gone. We lost by one point. It didn't feel like Christmas. Just another workday. The mood in the locker room was somber. We spoke about execution, about being mentally tougher than we were. Teams were roughing us up and getting into our heads. The referees were letting them. But more important, we were letting them.

Our next stretch was thankfully mostly at home, which we sorely needed. We did well, but I can't say that we were happy with most of our wins. We were seeing a trend forming. Teams were playing us physically, which we took as part of the game. But we could also see that we were letting close calls affect our mood throughout the game at times.

I was having a hard time knowing what to believe. I had to remember that we couldn't just blow every team out by 20 points, even though I could see that we had the team to do it. Steve Kerr had talked to us about this. This, in fact, was one of his most consistent messages: enjoy the moment, don't beat yourself up too much about mistakes. But I could be really cynical when measuring how well we played. All I could see is what we can improve on, what we did wrong, rather than what we did well. Trying to keep that in perspective was hard.

We still had another big test lying in wait for us that season. Kevin had not been back to OKC for a game since he'd made his announcement. It felt like a movie, some type of scripted thing where we were the villains. When we walked on the court to a cascade of boos, it was more like a wrestling match than a basketball game. Everything about it felt fake—as though all of us, the fans, the other team were just playing our parts.

But there were lot of real emotions, and security posted everywhere, which gave the whole thing an ominous undertone. In a pre-game presser, I happened to point out that basketball was something I wanted to enjoy doing, and situations like this made it hard. It's a fine line. I recognize that people emotionally invest in us because of what we do, and I'd had a conversation with a media member off the record before when he pointed out that the rabid, sometimes illogical nature of the fan base was what made our sport great. I could understand that. But on the other hand, here was Kevin Durant, a professional who had decided to go work for another company in his chosen field because he liked the opportunity better, and that meant we needed extra security when we came to town? Like our lives would actually be in danger because a grown man made a job decision in a sport that has no real-world consequences? It boggled the mind. It was Curt Flood all over again. Oklahoma City was the only arena in the nation where they prayed before the national anthem. And still we spent the entire game being told, "Fuck you," while armed guards made sure no one rushed the court.

About a month later, we lost a game in Minnesota. I tried to take it in stride, but it's hard. Losing bothers me. It bothers every athlete, but it bothered me more on this night. March 10, 2017. When you're playing on a team like Golden State, losing is a lot more frustrating than usual, because it never seems necessary for us. It never seems inevitable. After a game like the one we had that night, I walk to the locker room thinking about every single thing we did on the court that we should have done better. I think about lazy bounces, passes getting picked off for easy buckets on the other end. I think about blown defensive assignments, people forgetting where they were supposed to go on a switch. I think about guys going underneath a screen when they know damn well they were supposed to go over top. I think about the mistakes I made. I was supposed to switch up on the point guard, but I got caught out of position not once but twice. I can't let go of these moments. They play over and over in my head like a movie I don't really like watching but can't find the remote to turn it off.

Of course, we played a talented team. Of course, Minnesota is well coached. That's what you have to say after a game. The press is looking for those words, and if they don't hear them, exactly in that order, then it becomes a whole thing. The truth is, I feel like we should have won. We all feel that we should have won. But if you say, "We should have won," then the next day everyone on every media outlet is talking about how you attacked Minnesota. They are shoving your quote in their players' faces out of context and getting reactions. They are trying to stoke a fight between grown men about their jobs. They are trying to interject themselves in a relationship that they don't even understand. They don't understand how you have respect for those guys, how you played alongside them in camps and tournaments when you were fifteen, how they were rookies on your team when you were on your second contract. How you looked out for them, told them about the way the league works. They don't understand that you know a little bit about the other guy's background. You've heard about where they came from, what they overcame. You may not even like the kid, but you have respect for him because you know how he nearly killed himself to get here so that he wouldn't have to die some other much uglier and more tragic way. They don't know any of that. All they know is that here's these two black guys wearing opposing uniforms. And they've heard about "beef" from some hip-hop blog and they think this is how we interact. So they keep trying to make "beef" happen. And no matter what you say in reality, they are going to try to fold it into their fantasy of hyper-aggressive black men loud-talking one another. So you have to speak with them slowly. You have to keep your sentences simple, so simple that not even they can fuck it up.

So you have to say, "We played a talented team. They're well coached [which in this case they were]. And we made some mental errors." What you're not supposed to say is the truth: We're better. We are a better team. We won seventy-three games last season. No other team in the history of the NBA has done that. It's possible that no other team ever will. We have two of the greatest shooters in history. We are not just a good team. We are a great team. We are a smart team and a well-coached team. An experienced team. A championship team. When we're all in uniform and playing well, there is not a team on this earth that can beat us.

That's how it feels inside. Like we are a championship team who lost. And I don't like it. We can't win every single game. Obviously. I have to keep reminding myself. We can't win every single game. I have to say it under my breath during that long, quiet walk back to the visitors' locker room. My knees will ache in the morning. My jersey is soaked with sweat, but the hallway is drafty and cold and I suddenly feel underdressed. My body doesn't feel like my own. It feels like some kind of tool that I used to know how to use but suddenly forgot. We can't win every single game. I hate this. I don't like admitting it. But I hate this.

When I get back to the locker room, we don't have enough time to get dressed, shower, and mope around, trying to hide our anger and disappointment about going onto the floor in someone else's gym, in front of someone else's fans, and losing. Because the press is waiting for us. I want to stay in the shower forever. I want to slip out of a trapdoor in the back of the locker room and never speak to anyone again. It's not the questions, although that can be annoying too. It's really the way they pile up on you, pin you against the wall or your locker. A whole herd of people climbing over each other shoving mics into your face, shining lights on you, so you can't even fully see who they are. Dozens of them and one of you. You do it night after night, and it's fine. It comes with the job. You can't complain. It's just that sometimes, sometimes the way they talk to you, look at you, push up on you, you don't feel completely like a human being.

I had gotten into it with a ref during the game. Nothing serious, no ejections or technicals, but it had to be clear to anyone watching that something was happening. You can add this to the list of things you're not supposed to say: You can't say you're better than the other team. You can't say anything is annoying or hard, because you're getting paid, you're living the dream. And maybe the thing you really, really can't say is that the referees are human too. And that just as we players sometimes get caught up in the moment, so do they. You can't say that sometimes they bring personal bias into their work and make a bad call. You can't say that they might actually be human beings with thoughts and feelings and prejudices that sometimes cause them to make mistakes or color the way they see things. You actually get fined five figures for saying that in print.

So I won't say it here.

But let's instead say that there was a reason I was not in a great mood coming off the floor in Minnesota and it had to do with more than the fact that we lost a game we should have won. No matter how you slice it, you can't deny that the dynamics of race that happen in the world also happen on an NBA floor, given current race relations in the country. There are white referees whose behavior feels uncomfortably like that of overseers. Not everyone is like this. But there are people who are like this. People who seem, no matter how respectfully you talk to them, to take everything you say as a sign of disrespect. People who seem to want to control you and your emotions as though your whole body and mind somehow belonged to them. People who tell you not to look at them, who give you technicals for making eye contact. People who seem to suddenly call the game entirely differently when your team is winning. People who seem to think you're not smart enough to know exactly what's happening in the sport that you've played almost all your life. People who become impossibly offended and fragile when you call them on their bullshit. People who insult your intelligence. It happens enough that we all notice it. It happens enough that we are no longer doubting what we see. So yes. There was a reason I was not in a great mood when coming off the floor in Minnesota.

Oftentimes reporters say they like talking to me because I'm "smart"—whatever that means. They say I offer more in-depth analysis of the game and how we played. And on this night they asked me if I was worried. If I thought our team was in trouble. Because of one loss. Our record at this point in the season was 52-13. And they wanted to know if we were worried. I understand why they want to make a story out of it. They need to talk about something, and so everything you do on a team like this is under a microscope. But it also feels like they have a hard time accepting it if you tell them you're not worried. It's almost like they don't want you to be unbothered. They seem to take a certain amount of joy in seeing you suffer. Maybe it's just that they like the story. Maybe it's something else.

So they asked me if I was worried. And I thought about it for a moment. Not long enough, maybe. And I said, "What would a dumb nigga say?" I could feel the air in the room suddenly disappear. The reporter I was talking to was a black guy. The only one in the press scrum that evening. He started to giggle nervously. He was having a moment of double consciousness too. We try to act like race doesn't matter. We have to in order to get by, but sometimes I just don't feel like pretending. What would a dumb nigga say? "Just play harder. Figure it out. Ain't that what we used to say? Thankful for the opportunity."

We're not supposed to say that there are fucked-up things about the way this game is played. We're supposed to take the money and be quiet. We're supposed to be grateful that we've been given an opportunity to have wealth, to send our kids to private schools. And the exchange is that we aren't supposed to say anything about anyone. We're supposed to wait quietly.

I could tell they didn't know what to say next. I let the silence sit. It was kind of an out-of-body experience. I'd been playing this press game long enough, and I knew that what was coming out of my mouth right now was going to echo forever. There would be reactions and reactions to reactions. Pieces would be written. Sports-talk hosts would deliver lengthy monologues about how offended they were. White guys might burn my jersey. I didn't care. In that moment, I didn't care. I would care more later. And still later I would care less. But in that moment, I didn't care at all.

"Is it tougher to take losses like this when you come back?" asked a white guy, trying desperately to change the subject. "You guys fight back from seventeen, get ahead by one, and then lose it at the end?"

"No, losing is losing," I said. "Losing is losing." And that's the god's honest truth. Maybe I should have stopped there. Maybe I should have called the interview over, said the disingenuous, "Thank you, fellas," and walked away. But I've never been the kind of person to quit while I'm behind. There was one more question from the black guy.

"Was it planned that you guys would take tomorrow off?" He was talking about the game we had the next night. We were flying to San Antonio right after this presser, arriving at close to 2:00 a.m., getting to the hotel and sleeping a few hours, then practicing and getting ready for a 7:00 p.m. tip. There was talk from Coach of resting a few of us for that game. Of course I had heard about that. He asked me if I was OK with resting.

"I do what Master say" was how I replied.

Maybe I shouldn't have said it. A lot of people really, really thought I shouldn't have said it. Sometimes now I look back and think maybe I shouldn't have said it. But I did. You could hear a pin drop in the locker room. Reporters had that look on their faces like they were dogs gathered around a dining room table and I had let a choice piece of meat drop to the floor. They couldn't believe they were getting this on tape. I held my breath for just a moment. And waited. They complain about athletes always delivering clichés. Well, congratulations. Here's your non-cliché.

The interview ended soon after.

We got on a bus.

We got on a plane.

The night was colder than it should have been in March. Just below twenty degrees. We climbed aboard the flight, me feeling tired, defeated, and angry in the dark and cold, with bright airport lights shining in our faces, making silhouettes of our bodies; our breath forming clouds, floating up and disappearing into the night.

On the plane I thought about why I said what I said. Against my better judgment, I checked Twitter. I was already trending. I read a few comments. Some people thought it was funny, as I did. Most did not. I shut off my phone, put my head back, closed my eyes, and tried to put it out of my mind. Come tomorrow, this was going to be a whole fucking thing. Every black person paid to be in front of a camera for the next seventy-two hours would, by law, have to have an opinion on what I had said.

Why did I do it?

There are some young guys on our team. I think of them as little brothers. They are excited and eager and a little wet behind the ears. I love these guys. They know they've "made it." Some of them are just finished cashing their first checks. Some of them are still living in unfurnished apartments, driving rental cars around. That's how new this all is to them. I feel a great responsibility to these guys. I feel like I have a platform to talk about issues that they don't hear talked about very often. From the time you're little, all you hear about is how great it is to play in the NBA. I was talking with a young guy on the Celtics about this very issue. "Playing basketball for a living. You can't ask for much else," he told me. It makes sense, but when I think more about it, isn't this the attitude we're supposed to have? Just like we're not supposed to criticize the refs, just like we're not supposed to say we're a good team and we're also not supposed to ask for anything more than being basketball players. It's a rarified position. I'm one of four hundred or so men on the planet who gets to play in the NBA. I get paid more money than 99 percent of Americans. And a lot more money than 99 percent of black people. You can't ask for much else.

But we still have to live on Earth, don't we? We still have to face challenges. They see us as basketball players and that's all. But basketball is going to end one day for all of us. And how are we going to adjust to reality? I feel a responsibility to keep my guys, my rookies, and my teammates aware. I feel a responsibility to use my platform to help all of us understand what's going on.

I tried to sleep on the plane, but I couldn't. But it wasn't because I was thinking about what I'd said or how it would turn into days of bullshit. Though maybe I should have been. Shannon Sharpe would deliver a monologue on *First Take* the next morning about how I was unacceptable and ignorant. How I was disrespecting slavery and all our ancestors. I liked and respected Shannon. And I understood where he thought he was coming from. But still, it made me sad. He accused me of being "glib" and "cute." For some reason, it never occurred to him that I was angry. Sage Steele took the opportunity to say that no black person should use the word "nigga," because it makes us hypocrites. They even trotted out Jadakiss on some show to say that my words were unacceptable. The whole thing was just weird. But on the plane that night, I wasn't thinking about it.

I wasn't thinking about fines or what Coach Kerr might say. I knew he would be vaguely annoyed, but he would understand. I knew he'd have my back publicly. And I wasn't thinking about my teammates. I knew some of them would shake their heads and probably wouldn't like having to answer questions about my postgame comments while we had our hands full coming off back-to-back losses on a grueling road trip. I felt bad for putting them in that position, and I would say that, but I knew they would understand. They would laugh, they would get it. And we would be fine.

But when I closed my eyes on the plane, what I kept thinking about was one referee. And how he had looked at me at one moment during the game. Like I was nothing.

Trying to keep it light. Trying not to let that darkness take over me. Maybe we get into conspiracy theories too much, especially on the road. But maybe it's just part of human nature. Kevin Durant was averaging eight or nine free throws a game in Oklahoma City. In his first year with us, he averaged six. Steph, over his career, all with the Warriors, has averaged between four and five free throws per game, and I've watched him come into practice the next day with quarter-inch-deep gashes on his arms from plays that were not called. It's hard to imagine a back-to-back MVP, unanimous the second time, only getting to the line a handful of times per game like that. Most guys who average 30 points a game shoot way more free throws.

I recently had an assistant coach from another team text me after we played them. He and I went way back to my teenage years. He wanted to congratulate us on keeping our composure during the game. "What do you mean?" I asked. "Our game plan," he said, "is just to foul the shit out of you. We tell our guys every time-out, just foul the ball handler every time. We know they're not going to call it."

Even though this had been my sense all along, it was still surprising to hear it so obviously stated by someone else in the league. Why would this even be the case? Does the league feel like we're too good? Like we could just blow teams out, which would drive down viewership? Do they counter that by making us look beatable, like every team has a shot every night? It's crazy stuff. You can't call it a conspiracy. Still, when you love this game like I do, and you've watched it for as long as I have, it not only seems obvious, but it's maddening. When you think about the fans flipping you off, yelling at you in remote mountain towns while Trump is president. When the referees tell you not to make eye contact, and when you talk about it publicly and the response is a resounding "Quit whining. Take the money and shut up." It's maddening. You try to keep it light. You try not to get lost in all of it. It's crazy stuff, you tell yourself over and over again. Over and over again.

You also know that, as a team, many of your problems are of your own making. Just as a player might have a reputation that causes a referee to react more quickly to him than to someone else, we sometimes enter into a game with preconceived ideas about a particular referee. We may have had a history with him, or may have watched how he handled a particular situation in another game, and we may be bringing all that into the game as well. So the first time we disagree on a call, we are overreacting because we are putting it in context of everything else we think we know about him.

I can't tell if that was an easy season or a hard one. We breezed through the playoffs and beat Cleveland in five games.

09

Riding Home

t's game day. We are playing the Milwaukee Bucks, stumbling gracelessly, it feels, to the end of a long and bumpy season. Our record today is 58-17, which is good. But we're still the second seed in the West. Houston is the name on everyone's lips. They've added Chris Paul, and James Harden is, per usual, balling out of control. It looks like things are clicking for them. They're unified and motivated. There was in incident early in the season when they apparently tried to go to another team's locker room and fight them after the game. It's funny. We all had a good laugh over it because all of us have wanted to do that once or twice at least. It's playground stuff, but on a more serious note, it shows that this is a team that feels they can battle anyone, and when you combine that with talent, experience, and good coaching, then you have a team that can do some damage.

Nevertheless, we're not scared of Houston or anyone else. It's just that you can't go three feet this season without someone asking you if they're going to beat you in the conference finals. It gets old after a while. It's not that we mind the question, but we definitely mind what's underneath the question. People are discounting us. We've won the championship two out of the last three years. And the year we didn't win, we still went 73-9 and lost in the final minutes of game 7 of the finals. When you have that kind of success, two things happen. One is that you get really pissed when people discount you. We didn't win those trophies in a raffle. We won them by being the best team in the NBA. We won them by playing through injuries, showing up at 8:00 a.m. to look at film and lift, and going out on the floor and beating everyone that you put in front of us. So yes, we take it personally when people start talking about how it's over for us when we're still—last time I checked—reigning NBA champs.

The second thing that happens when you have that kind of success is that people start hoping for you to stumble. They start trying to make you stumble. Everyone loves a winner right up until they start winning too much. Just look at the New England Patriots. When Tom Brady was an underdog, a backup who took this long-losing team to a championship, it was the feel-good story of the year. Now, five championships later, they're the most hated team in the NFL. What did they do, other than win and keep winning? It's a tale as old as the written word: people like to build you up, and then they like to take you down. I don't know why it's like this, but it is. It didn't take long for the ground beneath us to change once we won that first championship in 2016. The narrative has been written that the Warriors are bad for the NBA because they are too good and create a competitive imbalance. You can see it in the way the press has changed the story on us over the past few years. Draymond used to be feisty, the heartbeat of the team. Now he's a loudmouth and a dirty player. Steph used to be everyone's perfect angel, the guy you want your kid to marry. Now he's cocky and needs to learn a lesson. The Warriors used to be the Little Team That Could, and now we're the Evil Empire. It makes sense. Writers can make a name off of trashing us, and teams can make a name off of beating us. This comes with the territory of winning. It's a good problem to have. We're the biggest story in basketball over the past three seasons, and now maybe the best part about it is that we get to be underdogs again. We get to have something to prove.

Shoot-around this morning is at 10:00 a.m. in the practice facility at the Marriott Hotel in downtown Oakland. I set my alarm for 7:50, planning to throw on some clothes and get to the facility at about 8:30. But I wake up and realize I'm far too tired to get up yet. I had a long day yesterday and didn't stop until about 12:45 a.m. I was with my son. I brought him to practice with me. We worked out together, made pizza in the backyard, shot some hoops, played golf, tossed these beanbags around. It was wonderful and also exhausting. By the time I got into bed, I was beat, and sleep fell over me like death. So this morning, I reset my alarm for 8:25, thinking I'd get to the weight room a little late but still with plenty of time to get some work in. When I next wake up, I can tell that something is wrong by the amount of light in the room. It is 9:00 a.m. Damn. I literally never sleep in for anything. That should have been my first sign that it's going to be one of those days.

I think about climbing out of bed, but it immediately feels like my whole body is made of cement. I stare at the ceiling and think about the fact that the human body was simply not meant to run up and down a court for eighty-two games. We have ways of making it work. Grit, science, training. Blood centrifuges. More science. But in the end, we're simply asking our muscles, bones, and joints to do something they have no business doing. I can feel it in my knees—both of them are as creaky as a cellar door. My hips, especially on the left side, dully throb. My back feels like there's about six pounds of gravel weighing down the base of my spine. And yet, it's not over. This insanely long season is not yet over. There's a game tonight. And another and another. Then we get to the playoffs. And that's when it gets serious.

I lie there for a moment, doing a slow inventory of every ache and pain, scanning my body for points of fatigue and discomfort. I'm already late, but this is not time wasted. At this point in my career, fourteen years in, my body is an entirely new thing. I'm learning on this day, as I do every day, how to go about my job, where I can push, and where I have to be careful. I can already see that I need to take it extra easy in shoot-around. Every joint is screaming to be heard. If I don't listen well enough, I won't make it through the night. I can see that my left knee is going to have a mind of its own today. I can see that I'll have to spend extra time icing it, and definitely get a nap in after practice.

In the car I'm listening to a book called *Sapiens: A Brief History of Humankind* by a historian named Yuval Noah Harari. It's less a history of humans and more a history of thought, of consciousness, an exploration of how it came to be that humans developed complete societies with millions of members, when even the most social of animals have only a couple hundred members in their groups. He talks about shared imagined realities like money and religion. Things that we just decide are important even though, in the most absolute sense, they are nothing. Like an NBA championship. Like thirty thousand people in a room screaming while you chase a round, bouncing ball up and down a wooden floor.

Walking into the facility, I feel a thousand years old. I've done this literally over a thousand times. Every game day since the beginning of my career—I've lost track. The sky is overcast, as it often is on Oakland mornings. I am parked on the facility roof. I can see gray clouds blanketing the town like wool. I am walking gingerly. Each step is a compromise.

I am an hour later to the facility than I usually am. On pretty much every game-day morning other than this one, I try to get in by 8:30 for a 10:00 a.m. practice. This gives me a chance to work out properly before stepping onto the floor. This morning, however, I kind of have to rush it, which I hate doing. The older you get in this game, the more time you need to do things properly. There are young guys on our team who can stroll in at 9:30, polishing off potato chips, a couple of waffles, and a chocolate milk, then run up to the weights, lift like crazy for half an hour, jog out to the floor, and run a practice at damn near full speed. Those days are long gone for me. I've had to learn how to take what I need from each moment slowly but surely. At my stage of the game, each minute is a precious resource.

I get some fruit and water and head into the training room to get the kinks rolled out. The trainer works on my knees, back, and hips. I have one hip that rises higher than the other, and over the years my body has compensated by putting extra pressure on my opposite knee and ankle, creating still more problems. I lie there letting the trainer handle me, massaging the ligaments and tendons, relieving the stress, addressing the swelling. I've had tendonitis in both my knees since I was in high school. Most times I don't even notice it. But today is different. Today I can feel every single bit of it.

I make my way into the weight room and lie down at the bench for my first sets. Before I start, I close my eyes. And breathe. I can feel every part of my body. My back against the cool fabric of the bench, my feet on the floor, chest rising and falling. I put my hands around the bar and let myself feel how cold it is, how the grooves are rough to the touch. I let my breathing slow down to near-death levels, and for a moment I'm not anywhere. I'm just here. I have to do this. Each rep has to be exactly right, clear and complete. I have to feel the weights, connect with them. I need to literally be present for each repetition, from beginning to end, feeling every muscle. I need to breathe correctly through each one of them, otherwise it's wasted energy. And I don't have energy to waste.

I finish, feeling just the tiniest bit more alive. I realize that I'm going to actually make it through this day.

At 10:00 a.m. exactly, the buzzer sounds, signaling that it's time for practice to begin. It is always unbelievably loud, but today it feels louder than usual. We file in and take seats in the chairs at the end of the court. It takes a while to settle down. Nick Young and Draymond are joking about a whether Dray can make a one-handed shot from where we are sitting. He tries and it bounces off the front of the rim. Everyone reacts while Dray yells that he's ready to go double or nothing. The coaches are setting up the screens for film study of our team for tonight, the Milwaukee Bucks.

Once the film session starts, the vibe changes. We're focused and quiet, looking at how to defend against them. Our coaches have a plan. Four outs, deuce and kicks and building walls. Draymond is on "the Greek Freak," Giannis Antetokounmpo, the six-foot-seven phenom who has been a staple of highlight reels all year. We're breaking down how each player on the team works. Khris Middleton likes to come off the push dribble. Jabari Parker likes to do his work in iso. Their second unit runs a lot of wheel.

I don't say a lot, but I'm taking it all in. Draymond, meanwhile, is like the A student of our defensive lessons. He's focused, taking notes. When the coaches come up with a scheme, they don't tell him; they ask him if he sees it the same way. This is one of my favorite parts of the job, that point when we're all focused watching each moment. This is the part where we get to be students. I love it.

We break up and go into groups to run things over. There are ten baskets in the gym, making up four courts with two baskets on the far ends. The music starts, "Birthday Song" by 2 Chainz featuring Kanye, and it is suddenly organized chaos. Shaun Livingston is talking with an assistant, working on offensive drills. Draymond is doing post moves with an assistant. Steph, still recovering from an ACL injury, is recording an assistant coach shooting threes with his phone. Zaza Pachulia is practicing mid-range jumpers.

Klay and I are doing mid-range catch-and-shoots. He has a brace on the thumb of his shooting hand, but that's not stopping him from knocking them down. I like shooting alongside him because he's so smooth with it that it kind of infects me. Next we practice doing a few dribbles and then getting to a spot. It's precision. Rock a little, dribble behind the back, two steps either left or right, step back, and shoot. Repetition. Precision. Next we do the same thing but with a fake crossover instead of a real one. Little shimmy, two steps right. Shoot. Next behind the back from just inside the three-point line. Next pure catch-and-shoots. "Green Onions" by Booker T & the MG's is playing. Now baseline jumpers. Now free throws. I've got a good sweat going.

Next we do what we call a five-one-oh drill, a kind of full-court game with just a few guys where we switch between playing offense and defense. A man guards you, then cuts, then you pass, then he runs the offensive set. I am going as slowly as I can until it's time for me to cut, which I do at full speed. It's the only thing I do at full speed. It's not that I need to do the drills for myself—I know this stuff inside and out. It's more that I need to do it to show the younger guys how to do it. We've got a young guy who always cuts at the wrong time. Just a second too early. So I make sure he sees me do it correctly. Every half second matters. You cut too soon and you jam up the lane. You cut too late and you don't lose your defender in time. If football is a game of inches, basketball is a game of instants. Everything is a read, and your job is to keep a space. If somebody leaves a spot, that means it should be taken. It must run with perfection, like the whole thing is a Swiss watch. Gears fitting into gears fitting into gears. "Sweetest Girl" by Trae featuring Lil Wayne is playing.

Now I'm back for more free throws. I've got a good lather going now, a good sweat. For a second I can remember what it's like to not be limited by the creaks, aches, and pains of a body that has crashed on hardwood for thirteen years straight. I know the feeling won't last, but it's good for now.

Practice is over, and as I leave the floor, I'm brought over to shake hands with a family. A father, mother, two kids—older boy, younger girl. I say hello, but have no idea who they are. So we exchange handshakes and first names. I head into the food room since I can't chill in the medical room. I'm trying to watch golf, but one of the trainers has commandeered the training-room TV for opening-day baseball. I take a seat in the food room and watch Lucy Li, a fifteen-year-old golfer who is a wonder to behold. She was the youngest player to ever qualify for the LPGA tour, and she's an actual dynamo. When I look at her, an underdog with a laser focus that has taken her to a level most players only dream of, I recognize something in her. Something that makes sense to me and motivates me.

Now, sitting down, the full weight of today's practice is sitting with me. I can feel my knees all over again. I get them wrapped in huge ice packs, and soon I'll be fully immersed in an ice bath. I've had tendonitis in my knees forever, but there are days like today when I can actually feel each tendon in my knee. I can see them in my mind's eye, throbbing red and hot.

The trainer comes in and asks me if I know who the family was that I was just introduced to. I do not. It's a family who lost their old-est in the Las Vegas shooting back in October 2017, when a gunman opened fire on a crowd attending a concert. Fifty-eight people died, and 851 people were injured, including a member of this family. In the silence after he leaves, I sit with that. My knees are throbbing, my left hip still hurts. And I feel incredibly fortunate to be here in this moment.

I leave the facility with that unique combination of exhaustion and euphoria that I get after a decent practice. The fog has lifted a little, and now from the rooftop parking lot I can make out Oakland's cranes in the distance. I stop for a moment to take it all in. The city below me, car horns, someone laughing, and the sound of a truck backing up. I watch a pigeon take off across the sky by itself until I can't see it anymore. This is one of those moments that feels like a blessing.

Now it's time to eat. It seems like a little thing, but it's maybe the most important decision I make during the day. This morning I weighed in at 217, which is two pounds under my ideal weight for the regular season. I do my best at 219, or maybe 220. Anything more than that and I start to feel it in my joints. Once I played at 227 and I was as strong as an ox, just plowing through people, finishing at the rim. It was like having a super power, but a short-lived one—227 was just impossible to sustain. When I'm below 219, it's harder for me to defend. Guys can push me around on the block, back me up, move me out of the way for rebounds. It helps to be over 220 to guard LeBron, but there's only one of him. I've been eating vegan for health reasons lately. But I can't go full vegan because it's impossible to stay at 219 that way. So I pick and choose my spots. Today I'll eat meat.

The rest of the day is about shutting down before tonight's game. I head back home to decompress. I'm watching *The Office*—season 5, episode 20 is where I left off. I usually have three or four shows I'm watching at any given time. *Atlanta, The Chi, Billions,* and *The Big Bang Theory* are in the rotation right now. I watch three episodes before I take a nap. I know that when I wake up, everything will be different. It will be game night.

I like to think of all my media, everything I intake, as being part of a project. Music-wise my project right now is Jay-Z. I'm listening to the entire canon all over again from the beginning. I'm on *Reasonable Doubt* tonight. I just let it play through on my way to games. Wherever it stops, I pick it back up on the next game day. Never in between. I work myself up. My time to the games is time to get my mind right, and music is the key. I'll also listen to Kendrick Lamar, Nipsey Hussle, and a few others. But in the end it always comes back to Jay-Z and Kendrick. There is a clarity, a directness and completeness, in those artists that I can't seem to find anywhere else.

I arrive at the arena at 5:15 p.m., walk into the entrance, past the metal detector, past the cameras that film us as we arrive. I have some friends with me, so I need to take some time to make sure their family passes are all set up. Security at Oracle gets more intense the closer we get to the end of the regular season. They are preparing for the playoffs and maybe even the conference finals, where reporters from all over the world descend on our hometown arena.

Once I've got my friends squared away with their badges, I'm off. They're going to have to be on their own for the next three hours, because I can't think about anything but this game. The routine is the same. A small meal. Stretching. Getting the kinks rolled out. Getting into my uniform and warm-ups. Press availability. Shoot-around.

Five shots from seven different spots on the floor. Layups, pull-ups. Jumpers. You can't move to the next spot if you miss the last one. The crowd is starting to fill in, but I don't notice it. A DJ is playing party tunes, but I don't notice it. The jumbotron is showing an episode of *Dre Days*, a show I've recently started doing with TNT. It's the one where me and JaVale McGee go to Big K.R.I.T.'s studio in Atlanta and I lay down tracks for the hook. It's one of my favorite episodes. But still I barely notice it, even though it's me on the jumbotron. All I can think about is playing. All I can think about is winning.

We tip off at 7:37 exactly, and from early on, I can tell something is off about this game. Milwaukee opens up on a 10–2 run. We miss a bunch of shots. JaVale misses a dunk off an alley-oop. But KD gets a three, and JaVale blocks Giannis on the other end, and we finally get to a time-out. I come in at about the five-minute mark in the first, and we've been able to tighten it up to an 18–16 game. My first play in, I pick up a turnover and we score on a fast break. Next trip down the floor, KD is fouled by Giannis on a three, and there's no call. It's only the beginning.

More substitutions. Nick Young and Zaza Pachulia come in. JaVale and the rookie point guard Quinn Cook, who has been turning heads stepping in for the injured Steph, have a seat. I'm mostly just trying to keep my man in front of me, but then I get Giannis on a switch. He is able to get a shot off on a turnaround layup. Damn, he's quick. On the other end, KD shakes his man but can't finish. On the defensive end we're all confused. I get caught on a rough screen by Giannis, and I bump into KD, who is trying to cut. I'm not tired exactly, but I don't feel energized. I do a quick scan of my body. Left knee is aching slightly but overall I'm OK. This is game seventy-four on the year. No one is 100 percent at this point except for the guys who just came up from the G League.

It is then that the turnovers start. A missed pass, a shot clock violation, bad dribbles. We're all doing it and it's frustrating. On top of that, it really feels tonight, more than most nights, that the referees are just letting us get smacked around. I don't know if it's true, but we start focusing on it. Maybe it's mental fatigue from a long season—everyone is limping to the end of the year at this point—but I can feel frustration seeping into our game and the tension is mounting. It's carried over from previous games and from previous seasons. We're still in the game, but it's definitely a grind. Nothing seems to be coming easy.

I get a steal and lead a fast break, but by the time I get down floor, there's already too much defensive congestion for me to convert. I dribble around waiting for my guys to set up, but in the meantime the ball gets poked out of bounds. While I'm setting up for the inbound, it occurs to me that when I was young, I would have been able to take all those guys to the hoop. Those days are over, I think to myself as I find David West under the basket for an easy two.

Other end of the floor, I'm trying to help on Giannis, and for a moment we have him trapped in a double against the baseline. But he somehow finds Brandon Jennings, who I was guarding and who drains a three. It just feels like this whole night is like this. Nothing is coming easy. The lights feel brighter, the music seems louder and more annoying. Draymond gets shoved on a drive, still makes the shot, and they call the foul on *him* somehow! It's 40–38, we're still down by 2. Frustration is mounting and so are the turnovers. Giannis gets another dunk off of one. Quinn Cook is getting it going; he hits a three and we're still in there. Thank God for young guys. They don't have any of the shit built up that we do. They're just happy to be here.

Meanwhile I'm guarding Jennings, he trips on his way to the basket, and I get called. I watch it again on the jumbotron and it's even more ridiculous. The crowd is starting to boo. I'm trying to keep it together.

We all are, but some of us are doing a better job than others. Six straight Warrior turnovers later, they have ended the half on a 14–2 run.

And then it gets bad. KD gets frustrated on a no-call as he drives to the basket and takes contact. He approaches the ref, who won't even make eye contact with him. KD loses it. "Call a foul!" (He may have thrown in some more colorful language.) And that's it. It's his second technical foul of the night. He is ejected from the game.

Now everything falls apart. A cascade of boos rains down from the stands. They replay it on the jumbotron and no one in the arena can believe it. The crowd is chanting, "Ref, you suck!" over and over. KD is pissed and stalks off down the tunnel shaking his head. This half can't end fast enough. We walk off the floor to a chorus of jeers. As we walk off, a Hawaiian dance troupe consisting of like three hundred people, mostly kids, is waiting to take the floor for the halftime show. People are still booing. The kids don't even look nervous. They just look ready. Like us, they've put hundreds of hours into preparing for this moment. Sometimes this job is so strange.

In the locker room a lot of stuff is said that I can't repeat here, but suffice it to say that no one is happy. Steve and the coaches are really great about keeping us focused on the game plan, focused on what we can control, and there's a lot of that. Our turnovers are insane, and we're losing guys altogether on defense. We *don't* look like a championship team. We are one, but we don't look like one.

When our first offensive possession of the second half is a turnover, and our second is an air ball, we're pretty sure things aren't going to get better. There are moments when we look like we're about to do something. Quinn hits a nice runner, Patrick McCaw finds Draymond for a great dunk. But more than that it's just like watching the game slip through our fingers. By the end of the third there's a 16–8 turnover differential favoring the Bucks.

I come back in at 4:46 in the third to relieve Draymond. We're behind 78–61 and things are starting to get out of hand. Nevertheless, Pat McCaw hits a three. We're going to keep fighting. If we can. Kevon Looney gets a jumper to fall. But still we're getting outscored 44–28 in the paint. I'm gonna try to make that right in a second here. I drive a few possessions later, back my man up, and try a little mid-range turnaround. It misses but the moment I land, I feel something. Sharp pain, left knee. Dammit. I'm trying to jog back up the court, but with every step it stings more than the last. The coaching staff can see me grimacing. At the next time-out, I'm out of the game.

By the end of the third, we are down 20 points. We lose. Obviously. The mood after the game is somber. Quiet. People are genuinely angry. We're taught to brush it off, focus on what we can control.

It's interesting how the narrative changes. All of our guys have been hurt. Klay, Steph. KD was back for less than one game before he got tossed. Draymond just missed a week with a bruised pelvis. You never want to blame anything on outside influences. You're only to say "we didn't play well enough," but the truth is that's what it was. Outside influences. We were a team tonight trying to figure out how to play in all our new and ever-changing combinations, trying to ward off fatigue and trying to keep mentally focused among feelings of frustration and exhaustion.

In 2015 we were "the team that played the game the right way." We were supposed to be young and exciting and getting people back into basketball. People were telling us that they hadn't watched the game in twenty years, but we were making it fun for them again. We were the good guys. And if you think about it, the fact that we became good was as much the result of freak occurrences as anything else. Remember that Steph's ankle was a significant problem in the first few years of his career. In 2011–12 he only played twenty-six games. He was considered a guy you would re-sign but probably not give a max contract to, because his health could potentially be a problem. But his contract remaining small allowed them to sign me. If Steph's ankle had been healthy those first few years, the entire Golden State roster might look different than it does today. At times it felt as though we were a team of destiny. Too many fluke things landed just right for us to have our success. We felt we were the good guys who had done things the right way.

But somehow over time we became, in the eyes of some, at least, the bad guys. Even before KD came, the tide was starting to turn for us. But somehow him coming to us sealed the deal, as if we were now evil. Everything is scrutinized under a microscope and people are seeking out reasons to vilify us.

It's the blessing and the curse. Once again. We take the paycheck, so we know it going in. And everything we've done is for the purpose of following our dreams and experiencing victory and success. But there is also a human element to it that no amount of money can erase. It just doesn't sit right when you know that the way millions of people think of you is influenced by very little that you actually do and much more by how you're portrayed. And it makes its way onto the court. We know that the scouting report on us for most teams is, essentially, rough them up. Knock them around. They're not going to get the calls.

This is more than just a profession for a lot of us. There are basketball purists on our team. People who have devoted their entire lives to learning and mastering every single wrinkle and facet of this game, and from that perspective it feels like a disservice is being done to the game itself. But if you voice your opinion about it, then somehow that makes you worse. No excuses. Just shut up and play.

You're supposed to keep it real. But not too real. You need to hold your tongue, not speak your actual truth, because fans only want part of you. Just the part that feeds their narrative. It all makes you feel like less than a person.

And yet. We do take the checks. So how do you balance that? The need to be a person with the calling of your profession to essentially shut up and play. Or if you do speak, to do so only within the boundaries set forth by the NBA. You have a platform. But you can't fully use it.

On nights like these, games like this one, the silence is heavier in the car on the way home. Everything feels darker. More lonely. I have to keep my mind from spinning downward and I don't always know how to. There are aches and pains and soreness and there is sweat and fatigue. But there is something else. A feeling of being free but trapped. Crowded and isolated at the very same time. I'm in a beautiful car. The engine is incredibly quiet, almost muted. I can hear every sound in my head, every thump of my heart. My body feels heavy. I've crossed through the tunnel into the hills where I live. And even though I know it's not true, it feels, somehow, like I'm the only car on this entire open highway, the only car moving on this long, slow, painful, and empty night. There will be another game. At this point that's the only consolation I have. And it feels like a sentence.

———

We won the 2018 championship in a sweep of the Cleveland Cavaliers. It was the hardest and the easiest one of all. The hardest because it was our fourth consecutive year in the finals and the fatigue was daunting, both mentally and physically. We all had significant injuries that year, and I ended up watching the Western Conference finals against Houston from the sidelines. I bumped knees with James Harden in game 3 and ended up missing the rest of what turned out to be a seven-game series.

It was an interesting experience to miss a series. I liked getting the chance to see the game from a different perspective, to talk to the young guys. But I also got to see how many people only cared about whether I played. It got to a point where people wouldn't even ask me how I was doing. They would just open up with, "So when are you coming back?" Every fan I ran into, even friends and acquaintances, were telling me about different remedies they had heard about. Our GM, Bob Myers, once told me that you can tell who your real friends are by how they treat you when they need something from you and how they treat you when they don't. I was happy to find during my injury that I had some good friends and some others who were not.

The finals series was short. We simply outmatched that version of the Cavaliers. LeBron played great, but we were too much for them. We were up by about 30 points with a whole quarter left to play at the end of game 4, and this time I just let it wash over me. I spoke to every member of my team. I told them how I loved them, how I respected them. I told Steph Curry how much he inspired me with his faith and his honesty and his immovable goodness. I've played alongside him for five years and I've never seen him blow up, never seen him lose his cool. I told KD that he was the most talented player I had ever seen. I told Coach Kerr that he had taught me the game like no one else had. One by one, I spoke with each member of this squad. This brotherhood. I told my young guys that I loved them, and I believed in them. I tried to do for them what older heads had done for me when I was coming up. And I got to tell them something that Steve Kerr had always told all of us. Enjoy this moment. Enjoy it.

t is the off-season again. My fourteenth. By this time, the rhythm of an NBA year is no longer something that exists only on a calendar. It lives, seemingly, in my bones. As odd as it sounds, it feels to me like the cycle really begins during the playoffs. Maybe it feels that way for me because that's when the obsessive focus really locks in. And maybe the obsessive focus is where I feel most like myself. During the playoffs, and especially the finals, you are nowhere but in the game. At home, you're in the game. In bed, you're in the game. Even on days off, you're thinking about every play that happened, how it unfolded, how it should have unfolded. What it is that you're going to do differently the next time you step onto the floor. You literally cannot think of another thing. You disappear into the game and into the quest for a ring. It consumes you and you welcome it.

Then, in a flash, it's over. You've won. The confetti, the champagne, the parades. A thousand text messages, a million phone calls. You can't believe it. You are numb, numb with disbelief, numb with fatigue, numb with the feeling that you've somehow managed to do a thing that the entire world saw. You are a world champion. Everyone who sees you greets you that way. "Whaddup, Champ?" You begin every text with your teammates like this: "Whaddup, Champ?" Your friends, your coaches, your cousins, your family all greet you by saying, "Whaddup, Champ?" And it's amazing. It's like the fireworks have exploded in the sky and you are just sitting there, watching the embers fall to earth, slowly, like a dream. You cannot move.

But then, slowly, it's over. The novelty fades away, the numbness fades away. The sky is empty and dark again. You realize that you have nothing to obsess over. But you try to enjoy it because that's what everyone tells you to do. You try to get a month, just one month, when you don't think about anything related to basketball. You want to just hang out with your kids. You want to travel with your family. You want to buy stuff that you've been thinking about buying. You want to get reconnected with your family, reacquainted with a schedule that doesn't involve 8:00 a.m. workouts and five out of seven days on the road. You take stock of your body, of the little tears and abrasions, strains and bruises, that occurred over the season. You schedule the medical interventions you need in order to get your body repaired. You feel like a stock car in the garage after a particularly brutal race. You are scheduling meetings to work on the investment projects, media projects, branding opportunities, licensing negotiations you are making in order to establish a foothold and some shelter in the market for your family and your people. You want to get things done. You want to take advantage. You want to rest and relax. You want to enjoy it. So you try. But then you look up and all of a sudden a month has passed. It's over. You have to get back to the gym.

It is early August and you are back on a court. You can feel the rest right away. Your legs are spry, your energy flowing. You remember why you loved this game and have loved it since you were a child. There is anticipation now. Everyone feels like this is going to be their year. You can't wait to prove yourself. Whatever happened last season is over. This year's gonna be great. For you. Specifically. You just know it. Every player in August just knows it.

It's just like the excitement of getting ready for a new year in school. You can't wait to see what classes you have, you can't wait to wear all your new outfits. You can't wait to show up on campus and show everyone how you've glowed up over the summer. That's the feeling of being in the gym in August. You can't wait for training camp to start. The off-season is over and it couldn't have happened soon enough. You've gone everywhere you wanted to go, bought everything you wanted to buy, went to the club, partied. It was fine. But this, this right here, is where you want to be.

Boom, there you are. Training camp. You're starting to get back into your rhythm. Now you're bursting at the seams. By the third day of camp you're thinking, "Man, get this shit over with. Let's go! When does the regular season start?" You can't wait until it's the first game. You have the calendar marked. You know where the big games are. The adrenaline gets you going from tip-off. You want to kill these guys. You're going to go off for 30 or 40 in the first game, that's a fact, and there's no doubt about it.

The season is off and running, and a picture is starting to form. Who's good this year, who's not. Your team is a contender. You've started off strong, made it through November, and you're into December. Thirty games have been played. Then one morning before shoot-around, as you get up and drag yourself to the bathroom, it suddenly dawns on you just how many games are in a regular season. I mean, you've played over a decade. You should know. But each year it comes as something of a surprise. You can't believe how exhausted you are. You can't believe how early it is. You just want to maintain. You decide you just want to make it to Christmas. That's every player's mantra: "Man, just let me make it till Christmas."

If your team is struggling, sitting at 11-19, you're just trying not to throw in the towel, not to give up on the season. If your team is looking good, you're trying not to get bored, trying not to let bad habits creep in and take root. January comes and you're relying on your bench. These guys need to help keep it together, because now you're thinking about guys needing rest for one game here and there. But you need the bench to hold it together for you, not only to win games, but also to keep the systems in place, the little things, the execution, the attention to detail.

Meanwhile as January and February drag on, you're trying to keep it together. The coaching staff is getting creative. Ping-Pong tournaments. Everyone, let's just take a break and go bowling. We're having class outside today, guys. Guys are starting to get on each other's nerves. Draymond is getting bored and now he's trolling people, getting on your nerves on purpose, pissing you off. "Draymond, I'm going to whoop your ass," you finally say. And then the very next game, you go out and play better than you have in weeks and there he is clapping at you in the locker room after the game. "See?! That's what I was trying to do!"

You finally make it to the All-Star break. And it couldn't have come soon enough. If you're on a winning team, fans are hating because you're not blowing everyone out of the gym by 50 points every night. If you're on a losing team, the arena is starting to empty out, people are giving away their season tickets, and you're looking down the barrel of a long, boring run till May. Over All-Star break you may go to the festivities, but you may just stay home. If you've been in the league long enough, there's nothing to see here. A bunch of parties and a bunch of noise. You just need to rest your bones and clear your mind. The season is about to start.

You come back from All-Star break and you have a team meeting. It's a simple one and a straightforward one. "Listen," you say, "all that bullshitting is out of the way. It begins now. We need to slowly but surely work our way to peak. We want to peak in April, May." And you can feel that everything is different. The practices are different, the coaching is different, the jokes are different. The rookies are looking around wondering what happened to the team they played on for the first half of the season. You come out of the All-Star break and you are ready to whoop anyone. You're locked in. You're dealing with injuries, everyone is missing games with this or that ailment, but the mood remains the same. Next man up, don't drop the ball.

Now the playoffs are here. Whatever intensity you had during the second half of the season was nothing. This is where the entire operation becomes a commando force. The scouting is entirely different. During the season the coaches are looking at other teams like, "Yeah, this guy goes to his right and they like to double-team here. Go get it." But during the playoffs, we are studying a man's whole lifestyle. We want to know what he had for breakfast and which hand he uses to open a door. The meetings are like strategy sessions. "Steph, what do you have?" Steph breaks down in phenomenal detail his scouting and approach to the defender. "Klay, what do you have?" Klay does the same. Me, Dray, David West, KD. Each player hasn't just thought about the opponent. We've studied them like you study a man who might kill you. The jokes are over. I remember Nick Young, who was in his first year with us, looking around after that first playoff meeting. "Damn!" he said, his eyes wide. "We about to win a championship!"

And you're back in the game 100 percent. At home you're in the game. In bed you're in the game. On days off you're only in the game. It consumes you. And you welcome it.

———

But there is a larger cycle. The last days before training camp begin to have a certain feel to them. The days are shortening, the nights are cooling, and you can tell it's almost time to return, that the summer is coming to an end. And just like that, there is a time you know when your career is coming to an end. The summers themselves are what is shortening, and your body is what is cooling. And though you've known your whole career that the day will come for us all, that we can't do it anymore, that Father Time is, in fact, undefeated, the realization still manages to sneak up on you somewhat. It's like you've spent all day making dinner for a guest, but you are still surprised when they actually show up. No one can predict when things are going to end. But every single one of us can predict that they will.

You hear the stories. When a guy retires, he has a midlife crisis, like six months out. I remember early in my career Antonio Davis broke it down for me. When every guy retires, they miss one thing. And it's always the same thing. The bus ride. You miss being with the fellas. Cracking jokes. Talking about how your family is doing. Talking about business and politics and relationships. You miss being a part of a campaign with a band of brothers. Of all these men who have come from all these different places. From fathers who were professional players and had trophy rooms at home filled with twinkling rings, jerseys stiff and framed, signed game balls with long beautiful stories attached that they tell you at night when it is long past your bedtime. Men who come from single mothers, fathers who were never around. Brothers and cousins in prisons and caskets. Roaches and rats. Drug addiction and cold-blooded murders. One chance to make it out, a chance for which they have willingly sacrificed everything. You miss being with men who came from small towns where no one ever thought you'd survive. From youth-league coaches who drilled in you the fundamentals since you were five years old. Not just the fundamentals of the game, but the fundamentals of life. How to show up, how to push yourself, how to become something better than what anyone could have imagined. How to become what God has laid out for you. You miss that. You miss being a man with a team, a man with a purpose. At least that's what I've heard.

Recently we moved to a new house. We had lived in the hills, where the streets were steep and winding, but we got a place farther away from the madness, where there is some nature and some flat, open trails that you can ride a bike on. Which is good thing. Because even though my son is eleven years old, he hadn't had a lot of practice riding a bike. The hills we lived in made it impossible, and I rarely had time to take him elsewhere to ride. I felt responsible for that. He remembered how to run a pick-and-roll. He remembered how to switch on defense and how to decide when to go over top or underneath a screen. He knew which coaches were good and bad, and he knew when the refs made terrible calls. He knew about vegan diets, bench presses, two-a-days, and media availability. He knew what it was like to ride in a championship parade, and he knew what it looked like when a grown man came home late at night with his body broken after having lost an entire season.

But one of the things he didn't know was how to ride a bike. So, this off-season, after we won our third championship in four years, I took some time to teach him. I hope that he and I can one day ride together, gaining speed on these open trails. Because at certain times of the year, if I let my critical eye go just enough, I can squint, and for a brief moment these California hills remind me of my childhood. And I can remember the feeling of running through empty fields in Springfield, a hundred miles of sky in either direction, playing as freely as I wanted to for as long as the sun would stand up in the sky. And it's nice, for a brief moment, to have that feeling back.

ACKNOWLEDGMENTS

This book started as an idea that involved many reflections and emotions. I want to thank Rudy Cline-Thomas for conceptualizing the project and thinking outside the box, knowing me well enough to understand that I would embrace this journey (sharing many articles paid off in more ways than we thought, as we found Carvell!).

Special thanks to Carvell Wallace for his patience and getting out my thoughts. Huge thanks to the Claremont Club and Spa in Berkeley for being so accommodating throughout my and Carvell's many sessions there.

Much appreciation to Cassidy Sachs and John Parsley at Dutton, Sylvie Carr at Fletcher & Company, Patience Ramsey, and Paulette Eastmond, for carrying the load and keeping this whole process on schedule and gathering all the materials and facts needed till completion.

To my Pyramid family (y'all know who y'all are!), thanks for all the encouragement and holding me accountable throughout this thing and believing in the vision! Also my U of A family and NBA family. All my coaches going back to Coach Sherman at Springfield Housing Authority. Two guys who I found myself looking up to at the "elderly age," Grant Hill and Michael Strahan, thank you for being an inspiration and setting the template for young black athletes.

Moms, aka Linda Shank, we did it! Thank you for raising me and making me the way I am! RIP Frank Sr. My three seeds constantly motivating me.

Most important, my wife, Christina, for all the sacrificing and understanding during all the constant madness. Appreciate and love you dearly! Thank YOU!

—Andre Iguodala

For Georgia and Ezra, my reasons for love and work.

—Carvell Wallace